Bound to stay open

Publisher's Note

Otabind (Ota-bind). This book has been bound using the patented Otabind process. You can open this book at any page, gently run your finger down the spine, and the pages will lie flat.

SHAKESPEARE'S

MACBETH

TOTAL STUDY EDITION

COLES EDITORIAL BOARD

SHAKESPEARE WAS NEVER MORE MEANINGFUL —

... than when read in Cole's "Total Study Edition." The introductory sections present background information about the author and his work that will help you read the play with understanding and appreciation. Efficient three-column arrangement of the complete text is convenient for the reader. Adjacent to the text there is a running commentary that provides clear supplementary discussion of the play as it develops. Obscure words and expressions used by Shakespeare are explained in the glosses directly opposite the line in which they occur. The numerous allusions are also clarified.

ISBN 0-7740-3200-6

© COPYRIGHT 1998 AND PUBLISHED BY
COLES PUBLISHING COMPANY
TORONTO - CANADA
PRINTED IN CANADA

Manufactured by Webcom Limited
Cover finish: Webcom's Exclusive **DURACOAT**

Macbeth

Contents

his Seruants.

an introduction

THE Tragicall Historie of HAMLET,
Prince of Denmarke.

By William Shakespeare.

Newly imprinted and enlarged to almost as much againe as it was, according to the true and perfect Coppie.

AT LONDON
Printed by I. R. for N. L. and are to be sold at his shoppe vnder Saint Dunstons Church in

SHAKESPEARE'S LIFE

The Early Years

Despite the scholarship it has generated, our knowledge of Shakespeare's life is sketchy, filled with more questions than answers, even after we discard the misinformation accumulated over the years. He was baptized on April 26, 1564, in Holy Trinity Church, Stratford-on-Avon. As it was customary to baptize children a few days after birth, he was probably born on April 23. The monument erected in Stratford states that he died on April 23, 1616.

William was the third child of John Shakespeare and Mary Arden, daughter of a wealthy land-owner. They married around 1557. Since John Shakespeare owned one house on Greenhill Street and two on Henley Street, it is not certain where William was born, though the Henley Street house draws many tourists each year.

2

William to Shakespeare

William's two older sisters died in infancy, but three brothers and two other sisters survived at least into childhood.

Shakespeare's father was well-to-do, dealing in farm products and wool, and owning considerable property in Stratford. After holding a series of minor municipal offices, he was elected alderman in 1565, high bailiff (roughly similar to the mayor of today) in 1568 and chief alderman in 1571. There are no records of young Will Shakespeare's education, but he probably attended the town school. Ben Johnson's line about Shakespeare's having "small *Latine*, and lesse *Greeke*" refers not to his education, but to his lack of indebtedness to the classical writers and dramatists.

When Shakespeare was eighteen years old he married Anne Hathaway. She was some years older than he, and the marriage seems to have been a hasty affair. Shortly after the marriage, Susanna, the first child, was born. Two years later, in 1585, twins Hamnet and Judith were baptized.

Theatrical Life

Shakespeare's years before and immediately after the time of his marriage are not charted, but rumour has him as an apprentice to a master butcher, as a country teacher or an actor with some provincial company. He is supposed to have run away from whatever he was doing for livelihood and to have gone to London, where he soon joined a theatrical group. At this time there were only two professional houses established in London, The Theatre (opened in 1576) and The Curtain (opened in 1577). His first connection with the theater was reputedly as holder of horses; that is, one of the stage crew, but a most inferior assignment. Thereafter, he became an actor, a writer and a director. Such experience had its mark in the theatricality of his plays. We do know that he was established in London by 1592, when Robert Greene complained in *A Groatsworth of Wit* (September, 1592) that professional actors had gained priority in the theater over university-trained writers like himself: "There is an upstart Crow, beautified with our feathers, that with his *Tygers hart wrapt in a Players hyde*, supposes he is as well able to bombast out a lanke verse as the best of you: and beeing an absolute *Iohannes fac totum* [Jack-of-all-trades], is in his owne conceit the onely Shake-scene in a countrey." An apology for Greene's ill-humoured statement by Henry Chettle, the editor of the pamphlet, appeared around December 1592, in *Kind-Hart's Dream*.

Family Affairs

To return to the known details of his family life, Shakespeare's son, Hamnet, was buried at Stratford on August 11, 1596; his father was given a coat of arms on October 20, 1596; and Will purchased New Place (a refurbished tourist attraction today) on May 4, 1597. The London playwright obviously had not severed connections with his birthplace, and he was reflecting his new affluence by being known as William Shakespeare of Stratford-upon-Avon, in the County of Warwick, Gentleman. His father was buried in Stratford on September 8, 1601, and his mother, on September 9, 1608. His daughter, Susanna, married Dr. John Hall on June 5, 1607, and they had a child named Elizabeth. His other daughter, Judith, married Thomas Quiney on February 10, 1616, without special licence, during Lent, and was, therefore, excommunicated. Shakespeare revised his will on March 25, 1616, leaving his second best bed to his wife. He died shortly afterwards and, according to the parish register, he was buried on April 25, 1616.

SHAKESPEARE'S WRITINGS

Order of Appearance

Dating of Shakespeare's early plays, while based on inconclusive evidence, has tended to hover around the early 1590s. Almost certainly, it is his chronicles of Henry the Sixth that Philip Henslowe, an important theatrical manager of the day, referred to in his diary as being performed during March-May, 1592. An allusion to these plays also occurs in Thomas Nashe's *Piers Penniless His Supplication to the Devil* (August, 1592).

3

Exterior view of "The Globe"

THAMESIS

Shakespeare's London

Interior view of "The Globe"

an introduction to Shakespeare

The first published work to come from Shakespeare's hand was *Venus and Adonis* (1593), a long poem, dedicated to Henry Wriothesley, Earl of Southampton. A year later, *The Rape of Lucrece* appeared, also dedicated to Southampton. Perhaps poetry was pursued during these years because the London theaters were closed as a result of an outbreak of plague. The *Sonnets*, published in 1609, may owe something to Southampton, who had become Shakepeare's patron. Perhaps some were written as early as the first few years of the 1590s. They were mentioned (along with a number of plays) in 1598 by Francis Meres in his *Palladis Tamia*, and sonnets 138 and 144 were printed without authority by William Jaggard in *The Passionate Pilgrim* (1599).

There is a record of a performance of *A Comedy of Errors* at Gray's Inn (one of the law colleges) on December 28, 1594, and during early 1595, Shakespeare was paid, along with the famous actors Richard Burbage and William Kempe, for performances before the queen by the Lord Chamberlain's Men, a theatrical company formed the year before. The company founded the Globe Theatre on the south side of the Thames in 1599 and became the King's Men when James I became king. Records show frequent payments to the company through its general manager, John Heminge. From 1595 through 1614

there are many references to real estate transactions and other legal matters, to many performances and to various publications connected with Shakespeare.

Order of Publication

The first plays to be printed were *Titus Andronicus*, around February, 1594, and the garbled versions of *Henry VI*, Parts II and III, in 1594. Thereafter, *Richard III* appeared in 1597 and 1598; *Richard II*, in 1597 and twice in 1598; *Romeo and Juliet*, in 1597 (a pirated edition) and 1599, and many others. Some of the plays appear in individual editions, with or without Shakespeare's name on the title page, but 18 are known only from their appearance in the first collected volume (the so-called First Folio) of 1623. The editors were Heminge and Henry Condell, another member of Shakespeare's company. *Pericles* was omitted from the First Folio although it had appeared in 1609, 1611 and 1619; it was added to the Third Folio in 1664.

There was a reluctance to publish plays at this time for various reasons: many plays were carelessly written for fast production; collaboration was frequent; plays were not really considered *reading* matter; they were sometimes circulated in manuscript; and the theatrical company, not the author, owned the rights. Those plays given individual publication appeared in a quarto, so named from the size of

4

FLUVIUS

South warke

the page. A single sheet of paper was folded twice to make four leaves (thus *quarto*) or eight pages; these four leaves constitute one signature (one section of a bound book).

Authorized publication occurred when a company disbanded, when money was needed but rights were to be retained, when a play failed or ran into licensing difficulties (thus, hopefully, the printed work would justify the play against the criticism), or when a play had been pirated. Authorized editions are called good quartos. Piratical publication might occur when the manuscript of a play had circulated privately, when a member of a company desired money for himself, or when a stenographer or memorizer took the play down in the theater (such a version was recognizable by inclusion of stage directions derived from an eyewitness, by garbled sections, etc.). Pirated editions are called bad quartos. There are at least five bad quartos of Shakespeare's plays.

Authenticity of Works
Usually, 37 plays are printed in modern collections of Shakespeare's works, but some recent scholars have urged the addition of two more: *Edward III* and *Two Noble Kinsmen*. At times, six of the generally accepted plays have been questioned: *Henry VI*, Parts I, II and III, *Timon of Athens, Pericles* and *Henry VIII*. The first four are usually accepted today, but if Shakespeare did not write

these plays in their entirety, he certainly wrote parts of them. Of course, collaboration in those days was common. Aside from the two long narrative poems already mentioned and the sonnets (nos. 1-152, but not nos. 153-154), Shakespeare's poetic output is uncertain. *The Passionate Pilgrim* (1599) contains only five authenticated poems (two sonnets and three verses from *Love's Labour's Lost*), and *The Phoenix and the Turtle* (1601) may be his, but the authenticity of *A Lover's Complaint* is highly questionable.

SHAKESPEARE'S ENGLAND

The world of Elizabethan and Jacobean England was a world of growth and change. The great increase in the middle class, and in the population as a whole, demanded a new economy and means of livelihood, a new instrument of government (one recognizing "rights" and changed class structure), a new social code and a broad base of entertainment. The invention of printing a century before had contributed to that broader base, but it was the theater that supplied the more immediate needs of the greatest numbers. The theater grew and along with it came less educated, more money-conscious writers, who gave the people what they wanted: entertainment. But Shakespeare, having passed through a brief period of amateur writing, proceeded to set

down important ideas in memorable language throughout most of his career. His plays, particularly the later ones, have been analyzed by recent critics in terms of literary quality through their metaphor, verse line, relationships with psychology and myth, and elaborate structure. Yet Shakespeare was a man of the stage, and the plays were written to be performed. Only this will fully account for the humour of a deadly serious play like *Hamlet* or the spectacle of a *Coriolanus*.

Life in London
During Shakespeare's early years there, London was a walled city of about 200,000, with seven gates providing access to the city from the east, north and west. It was geographically small and criss-crossed by narrow, little streets and lanes. The various wards each had a parish church that dominated the life of the close-knit community. To the south and outside were slums and the haunts of criminal types, and farther out were the agricultural lands and huge estates. As the population increased and the central area declined, the fashionable people of the city moved toward the west, where the palace of Westminster lay. Houses were generally rented out floor by floor and sometimes room by room. Slums were common within the city, too, though close to pleasant enough streets and squares. "Merrie Olde England" was not really clean, nor were its people, for in those days

Queen Elizabeth

Elizabethan types

Lute, standing cup, stoop

there were no sewers or drains except the gutter in the middle of the street, into which garbage would be emptied to be floated off by the rain. Plague was particularly ravaging from 1592 to 1594 (when the theaters were closed to avoid contamination) and 1603. Medical knowledge, of course, was slight; ills were "cured" by amputation, leeching and bloodletting. The city was (and still is) dominated by St. Paul's Cathedral, around which booksellers clustered on Paternoster Row.

Religious Atmosphere

Of great significance for the times was religion. Under Elizabeth, a state church had developed. It was Protestant in nature and was called Anglican (or today, Episcopalian), but it had arisen from Henry VIII's break with the pope and from a compromise with the Roman Catholics, who had gained power under Mary Tudor.

The Church of England was headed by the Archbishop of Canterbury, who was to be an increasingly important figure in the early part of the 17th century. There were also many schismatic groups, which generally desired further departures from Roman Catholicism. Calvinists were perhaps the most numerous and important of the Protestant groups. The Puritans, who were Calvinist, wanted to "purify" the church of ritual and certain ideas, but during the 1590s they were labeled as extremists in dress and conduct.

Political Milieu

During Shakespeare's lifetime there were two monarchs: Elizabeth I, 1558-1603, and James I, 1603-1625. Elizabeth was the daughter of Henry VIII and Anne Boleyn, his second wife, who was executed in 1536. After Henry's death, his son by his third wife, Jane Seymour (who died in 1537), reigned as Edward VI. He was followed by Mary Tudor, daughter of Henry's first wife, Catherine of Aragon. Mary was a Roman Catholic, who tried to put down religious dissension by persecution of both Protestants and Catholics.

Elizabeth's reign was troubled by many offers of marriage, particularly from Spanish and French nobles — all Roman Catholic — and by the people's concern for an heir to the throne. English suitors generally cancelled one another out by intrigue or aggressiveness. One of the most prominent was the Earl of Essex, Robert Devereux, who fell in and out of favour. He apparently attempted to take over the reins of control, only to be captured, imprisoned and executed in February, 1601. One claimant to the throne was Mary of Scotland, a Roman Catholic and widow of Francis II of France. She was the second cousin of Elizabeth, tracing her claim through her grandmother, who was Henry VIII's sister. Finally, settlement came with Elizabeth's acceptance of Mary's son as heir apparent,

though Mary was to be captured, tried and executed for treason in 1587. Mary had abdicated the throne of Scotland in 1567 in favour of her son, James VI. His ascent to the throne of England in 1603 as James I joined the two kingdoms for the first time, although Scotland during the 17th century often acted independently of England.

Contemporary Events

Political and religious problems were intermingled in the well-known Gunpowder Plot. Angry over fines that were levied upon those not attending Church of England services — primarily Roman Catholics — and offended by difficulties over papal envoys, a group of Catholics plotted to blow up Parliament, and James with it, at its first session on November 5, 1605. A cache of gunpowder was stored in the cellar, guarded by various conspirators, among them Guy Fawkes. The plot was discovered before it could be carried out and Fawkes, on duty at the time, was arrested. The execution of the plotters and the triumph of the anti-Papists led in succeeding years to celebrations in the streets and the hanging of Fawkes in effigy.

Among the most noteworthy public events during these times were the wars with the Spanish, which included the defeat of the Spanish Armada in 1588, the battle in the Lowlands in 1590-1594, the expedition to Cadiz under Essex in 1596 and the expedition to the

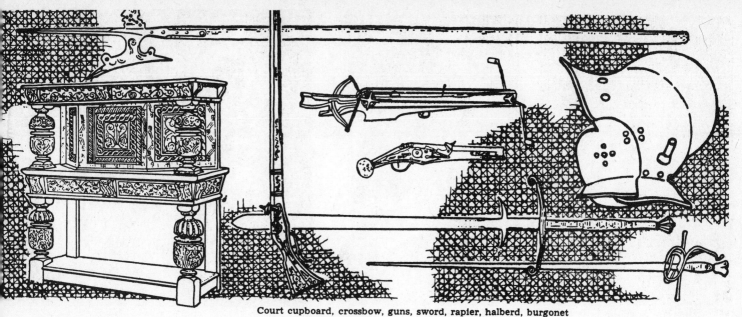

Court cupboard, crossbow, guns, sword, rapier, halberd, burgonet

Azores (the Islands Expedition), also under Essex, in 1597. With trading companies specially set up for colonization and exploitation, travel excited the imagination of the people: here was a new way of life, here were new customs brought back by the sailors and merchants, here was a new world to explore.

In all, the years from 1590 to 1601 were trying ones for the English people, relieved only by the news from abroad, the new affluence and the hope for the future under James. Writers of the period frequently reflect, however, the disillusionment and sadness of those difficult times.

THE ELIZABETHAN THEATER

Appearance

The Elizabethan playhouse developed from the medieval inn with its rooms grouped around a courtyard into which a stage was built. This pattern was used in The Theatre, built by James Burbage in 1576: a square frame building (later round or octagonal) with a square yard, three tiers of galleries, each jutting out over the one below, and a stage extending into the middle of the yard, where people stood or sat on improvised seats. There was no cover over the yard or stage, and lighting was therefore natural. Performances were held in the afternoon.

Other theaters were constructed over the years: The Curtain in 1577, The Rose in 1587, The Swan in 1595, and Shakespeare's playhouse, The Globe, in 1599. There is still some question about the exact dimensions of this house, but it seems to have been octagonal, each side measuring about 36 feet, with an over-all diameter of 84 feet. It was about 33 feet to the eaves, and the yard was 56 feet in diameter. Three sides were used for backstage and to serve the needs of the players. The stage jutted out into the audience and there was no curtain. The spectators often became part of the action. Obviously, the actors' asides and soliloquies were effective under these conditions.

There was no real scenery and there were only a few major props. Thus, the lines of the play had to reveal locations and movement, changes in time or place, etc. In this way, too, it was easier to establish a nonrealistic setting, for all settings were created in words. On either side of the stage were doors, within the flooring were trapdoors (for entrance of ghosts, etc.), and behind the main stage was the inner stage or recess. Here, indoor scenes (such as a court or a bedchamber) were played, and some props could be used because the inner stage was usually concealed by a curtain when not in use. It might also have served to hide someone behind the ever-present arras (hanging tapestry), like Polonius in *Hamlet*. The "chamber" was on the second level, with windows and a balcony. On the third level was another chamber, primarily for musicians.

Actors

An acting company such as the Lord Chamberlain's Men was a fellowship of ten to 15 sharers with some ten to 12 extras, three or four boys (often to play women's roles) who might become full sharers and stagehands. There were rival companies, each with its leading dramatist and leading tragic actor and clown. The Lord Admiral's Men, organized in 1594, boasted Ben Jonson and the tragedian, Edward Alleyn. Some of the rivalry of this War of the Theaters is reflected in the speeches of Hamlet, who comments on the ascendancy and unwarranted popularity of the children's companies (like the Children of Blackfriars) in the late 1590s.

The company dramatist, of course, had to think in terms of the members of his company as he wrote his play. He had to make use of the physical features and particular talents of the actors, making sure, besides, that there was a role for each member. The fact that women's parts were taken by boys imposed obvious limitations on the range of action. Accordingly, we often find women characters impersonating men. For example, Robert Goffe played Portia in *The Merchant of Venice*, and Portia impersonates a male lawyer in the important trial scene. Goffe also played Juliet, Anne in *Richard III* and Oberon in *A Midsummer Night's Dream*. The influence of an actor on the playwright can be seen, on the one hand, by

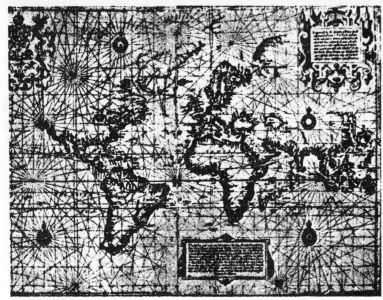

The world as known in 1600

Elizabethan coins

noting the "humour" characters portrayed so well by Thomas Pope, who was a choleric Mercutio in *Romeo*, a melancholic Jaques in *As You Like It* and a sanguinary Falstaff in *Henry IV*, Part 1; and by comparing, on the other hand, the clown, Bottom, in *A Midsummer Night's Dream*, played in a frolicsome manner by William Kempe, with the clown, Feste, in *Twelfth Night*, sung and danced by Robert Armin. Obviously, too, if a certain kind of character was not available within the company, then that kind of character could not be written into the play. The approach was decidely different from ours today, where the play almost always comes first and the casting of roles second. The plays were performed in a repertory system, with a different play each afternoon. The average life of a play was about ten performances.

SHAKESPEARE'S ARTISTRY

Plots

Generally, a Shakespearean play has two plots: a main plot and a subplot. The subplot reflects the main plot and is often concerned with minor or inferior characters. Two contrasting examples will illustrate this. In *King Lear*, Lear and his daughters furnish the characters for the main plot of filial love and ingratitude. Gloucester and his sons enact the same theme in the subplot. Lear and Gloucester both learn that outward signs of love may be false. In

A Midsummer Night's Dream, the town workmen (Quince, Bottom *et al.*) put on a tragic play in such a hilarious way that it turns the subject of the play — love so strong that the hero will kill himself if his loved one dies first — into farce, but this, in the main plot, is the "serious" plight of the four mixed-up lovers. In both examples Shakespeare has reinforced his points by subplots dealing with the same subject as the main plot.

Sources

The plots of the Elizabethan plays were usually adapted from other sources. Originality was not the sought quality; a kind of variation on a theme was. It was felt that one could better evaluate the playwright's worth by seeing what he did with a familiar tale. What he stressed, how he stressed it, how he restructured the familiar elements — these were the important matters. Shakespeare closely followed Sir Thomas North's popular translation of Plutarch's *Life of Marcus Antonius*, for example, in writing *Antony and Cleopatra*. He modified Robert Greene's *Pandosto* and combined it with the Pygmalion myth in *The Winter's Tale*, while drawing the character of Autolycus from certain pamphlets written by Greene. The only plays for which sources have not been clearly determined are *Love's Labour's Lost* (probably based on contemporary events) and *The Tempest* (possibly based on some shipwreck account from travellers to the New World).

Verse and Prose

There is a mixture of verse and prose in the plays, partially because plays fully in verse were out of fashion. Greater variety could thus be achieved, and character or atmosphere could be more precisely portrayed. Elevated passages, philosophically significant ideas and speeches by men of high rank are in verse, but comic and light parts, speeches including dialect or broken English, and scenes that move more rapidly or simply give mundane information are in prose. The poetry is almost always blank verse (iambic pentameter lines without rhyme). Rhyme is used, however (particularly the couplet), to mark the close of scenes or an important action. Rhyme also serves as a cue for the entrance of another actor or some off-stage business, to point to a change of mood or thought, as a forceful opening after a passage of prose, to convey excitement, passion or sentimentality, and to distinguish characters.

Shakespeare's plays may be divided into three general categories, though some plays are not easily classified and further subdivisions may be suggested within a category.

History

The history play, or chronicle, may tend to tragedy, like *Richard II*, or to comedy, like *Henry IV*, Part I. It is a chronicle of some royal personage, often altered for

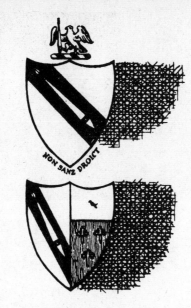

Wood cut camp illustration

Shakespeare's Coat of Arms

dramatic purposes, even to the point of falsifying the facts. Its popularity may have resulted from the rise of nationalism, nurtured by the successes against the Spanish, the developing trade and colonization, and England's rising prestige as a world power. The chronicle was considered a political guide, like the popular *Mirror for Magistrates*, a collection of writings showing what happens when an important leader falls through some error in his ways, his thinking or his personality. Thus, the history play counsels the right path by negative, if not positive, means. Accordingly, it is difficult to call *Richard II* a tragedy, since Richard was wrong and his wrongness harmed his people.

Tragedy

Tragedy, in simple terms, means that the protagonist dies. Certain concepts drawn from Aristotle's *Poetics* require a tragic hero of high standing, who must oppose some conflicting force, either external or internal. The tragic hero should be dominated by a *hamartia* (a so-called tragic flaw, but really an *excess* of some character trait, e.g., pride), and it is this *hamartia* that leads to his downfall and, because of his status, to the downfall of others. The action presented in the tragedy must be recognizable to the audience as real. Through seeing it enacted, the audience has its passion (emotions) raised, and the conclusion of the action thus

brings release from that passion (*catharsis*). A more meaningful way of looking at tragedy in the Elizabethan theater, however, is to see it as that which occurs when essential good (like Hamlet) is wasted (through disaster or death) in the process of driving out evil (such as Claudius represents).

Comedy

Comedy, in simple terms, means that the play ends happily for the protagonists. Sometimes the comedy depends on exaggerations of man's eccentricities — comedy of humours; sometimes the comedy is romantic and far-fetched. The romantic comedy was usually based on a mix-up in events or confused identity of characters, particularly by disguise. It moves towards tragedy in that an important person might die and the mix-up might never be unravelled. But, in the nick of time, something happens or someone appears (sometimes illogically or unexpectedly) and saves the day. It reflects the structure of myth by moving from happiness to despair to resurrection. *The Winter's Tale* is a perfect example of this, for the happiness of the first part disappears with Hermione's exile and Perdita's abandonment. Tragedy is near when the lost baby, Perdita, cannot be found and Hermione is presumed dead. But Perdita reappears, as does Hermione — a statue that suddenly comes to life. Lost identities are established and confusions disappear, but the mythic-comic nature of the play is

seen in the reuniting of the mother, Hermione, a kind of Ceres, with her daughter, Perdita, a kind of Proserpina. Spring returns, summer will bring the harvest, and the winter of the tale is left behind — for a little while.

What is it, then, that makes Shakespeare's art so great? Perhaps we see in it a whole spectrum of humanity, treated impersonally, but with kindness and understanding. We seldom meet in Shakespeare a weeping philosopher: he may criticize, but he criticizes both sides. After he has done so, he gives the impression of saying, Well, that's the way life is; people will always be like that — don't get upset about it. This is probably the key to the Duke's behaviour in *Measure for Measure* — a most unbitter comedy despite former labels. Only in *Hamlet* does Shakepeare not seem to fit this statement; it is the one play that Shakespeare, the person, enters.

As we grow older and our range of experience widens, so, too, does Shakespeare's range seem to expand. Perhaps this lies in the ambiguities of his own materials, which allow for numerous individual readings. We meet our own experiences — and they are ours alone, we think — expressed in phrases that we thought our own or of our own discovery. What makes Shakespeare's art so great, then, is his ability to say so much to so many people in such memorable language. He is "the show and gaze o' the time."

Inverness Scotland landscape

an introduction to The Trag

The following introduction will discuss in general terms some of the chief facts and problems concerning *The Tragedy of Macbeth* itself and its history. It will thus both supplement the more detailed comments beside the text, and lend more unity to them.

DATE OF COMPOSITION

The Tragedy of Macbeth was printed in 1623, in the First Folio. This famous edition was published by Heminge and Condell, two actor-colleagues of Shakespeare's, and is a collection, the first, of the playwright's works. All our later printings stem from this original. The earliest definite mention of a performance occurs in a book of plays (a sort of theater-goer's diary) written by the physician and astrologer, Simon Forman, who saw *Macbeth* at the Globe theater on April 20, 1611. On the other hand, the connection of the play with King James I (see below) makes it inconceivable that the play could have been written earlier than his coming to the throne in 1603. The more accurate dating of the play within the period 1603-11, is a matter of intelligent guesswork. Most scholars agree that the play must have been written during the year 1606. There are several reasons for assigning this date. First, *King Lear*, which resembles *Macbeth* in style and mood, was performed as early as 1606. Second, there are many references in the play which apply to such public

events of the years 1605-6 as the Gunpowder Plot, King James's visit to Oxford University, and the royal visit of Christian IV of Denmark. While none of these by itself would be conclusive, there is a sufficient cluster of them to be significant. (Most of them are noticed in the comments beside the text.)

THE FIRST FOLIO TEXT

Macbeth, as it has descended to us from the First Folio, is the shortest (with the exception of *The Tempest*) of the major plays. Besides this brevity, it is also a curiously imperfect play, containing many improbabilities especially with regard to the lapse of time and the sequence of events. These would bother readers more than they do if they were not offset by the play's positive qualities of tragic grandeur, psychological depth, and poetic power. It is illogical, for instance, that Macbeth in what appears to be a matter of months from Duncan's death, should have ruined his country and reached old age. It is improbable that Lennox and the other lords should know of Macduff's flight to England before Macbeth does (III, vi and IV, i), in spite of the latter's spy system.

Besides these flaws, the play shows signs of having been doctored for a performance with spectacular stage effects added, notably the two appearances of Hecate (III,v and IV,i) with their accompanying songs and dances of the witches (by

Thomas Middleton). It is hard to say what the extent of this alteration was. Was the play shortened by drastic cuttings? Were the scenes rearranged from their original order? Possibly: it is not known. It is true that plays were in those days usually the property of the company rather than the author, that Shakespeare around the years 1608-10 began to spend an increasing proportion of his time in Stratford rather than London, that his company of actors began producing plays in the indoor theater at Blackfriars (where stage spectacle was possible on a grand scale) in 1609, and that popular taste for lavish and showy stage effects was growing steadily from 1604-05 until well past the period we are concerned with.

JAMES I and MACBETH

When James VI of Scotland became James I of England in 1603, both courtiers and populace gave him a heartfelt welcome. They had been very anxious as the end of Queen Elizabeth's reign approached and the question of her successor was not settled. Consequently the speedy and peaceful installation of James I was a great relief to the nation. Plays tactfully complimentary to the new monarch would at once encourage his friendly regard and accord with public sentiment. But Shakespeare and his companions had a more personal reason to honor the king. Shortly after his coming to the throne, on May 19,

three weird sisters

y of Macbeth

1603, he had taken them under his personal patronage, changing their name from the Lord Chamberlain's Servants to the King's Servants. He called frequently for their appearance at his court, gave them special privileges in their public dealings, and helped them with grants of money when the plague closed the theaters.

In order to understand the extent of *Macbeth's* relevance to King James, we must first learn more about the king's beliefs. First of all he was a scholar of some reputation, his chief subjects being theology and what we should now call political science. He was well-read in literature also and he wrote both poetry and a series of theoretical works on his favorite subjects.

In religion he was a Protestant of very strict faith, and counted upon the supernatural influence of God upon human affairs. This bias influenced his theory of kingship and government, and was the root of his curious and minute interest in witchcraft as material evidence for the existence of supernatural evil. He believed that witches and magicians were agents of the devil; that the devil was permitted by God to work upon men as a punishment to the wicked, and a temptation to test the faith of the virtuous. Thus a man faced with Satan's temptation would be faced with a choice, and on the basis of that choice he would be judged. Both Macbeth and Banquo are so tested in the play. He believed that God distin-

guished kings from ordinary men and dealt differently with them, that they were chosen by God as his lieutenants and formed to rule according to His will and wisdom for the well being of the whole state. Thus Malcolm is the rightful heir to the throne by "due of birth," and Macbeth's crime is in a double sense a crime against God in usurping the places of his chosen rulers.

James's own statements of some of these beliefs were available to Shakespeare in book form. Three of his works, previously printed in Scotland, were reissued in London in 1603. They are: *News From Scotland* (an account of the trial, at which the king had presided, of a coven of Scottish witches from Forres who had tried to secure James's death through shipwreck during his voyage to Denmark in 1589), *Daemonologie* (a treatise on witchcraft and magic describing how witches operated and outlining their connections with the devil), and *Basilikon Doron*, or the kingly gift, (a work written for the instruction of his son as to the rights and duties of a Christian king). Perhaps the greatest of Shakespeare's compliments to his king resides in his basing so much of the theme of the play upon the king's ideas, but if so it is not the most pointed one.

No less than five of the virtuous characters in *Macbeth* are direct ancestors of King James: Duncan, Malcolm, Siward, Banquo, and Fleance. In view

of James I's own belief in the rightness of hereditary succession to the throne, it is pertinent to notice two further points. First, owing to the marriage of James IV of Scotland to the daughter of Henry VII, James had a hereditary claim to the English throne. Second, at the time of King Duncan, the law of hereditary succession in Scotland was only three generations old.

Before the reign of Duncan's great grandfather, Scottish Princes of Cumberland had been elected by the council of thanes. This council was not altogether happy with the new order, and its establishment was not yet firm. Thus the moment is highly dramatic when Duncan proclaims Malcolm the Prince of Cumberland, according to the new law, because Macbeth himself was eligible by blood and capacity, and was the most likely candidate for election by the thanes had the older custom been followed.

SOURCES FOR THE STORY

Although Shakespeare may have taken his lead for the creation of Macbeth's character from the version of the story in George Buchanan's *Rerum Scoticarum Historae*, his chief source was in Holinshed's *Chronicles of England, Scotland, and Ireland*. But he made several changes in this original, some in the interest of making a stronger and more unified play, some apparently in order to present James

The wood of Birnam

I's ancestors in a better light. For instance: Banquo in the history was Macbeth's accomplice in Duncan's murder. Banquo was himself murdered on his way home from Macbeth's feast (a course of action that would make the banquet scene as we have it impossible). Macbeth ruled Scotland for ten years virtuously and well, according to Holinshed, before turning to tyranny. Duncan was a very young and excessively weak king. The circumstances of Duncan's murder were taken not from his own story, but the earlier and parallel story of King Duffe which was much more dramatic and more suitable to the advanced age of Shakespeare's Duncan. The chronicle has three different sources for the prophecies, the three goddesses of destiny, a magician, and a witch. A similar dramatic telescoping of events occurs in the case of Sweno's invasion. The chronicle has two successive attacks; Sweno was followed by Canute, and it was Canute who was forced by Macbeth to pay tribute for permission to bury his dead on Inchcolm.

an introduction
to the Tragedy
of Macbeth

THE NATURE OF TRAGEDY

The whole range of dramatic expression of human life is bordered by the two great types of tragedy and comedy, a fact often symbolized by the two masks, one weeping and the other laughing, which frequently decorate theaters, playbooks, and programs. Tragedy deals with life's bitterness and defeat, and high tragedy with the extreme possibilities of these feelings. Now as each age of history has its own fundamental beliefs and values, so each has its own ideas of what life's greatest bitterness must be; hence the definition of tragedy, from time to time, has had to be revised.

In England just before Shakespeare's time, a rather simple and broad definition was accepted, based on the age old idea of Fortune's Wheel which, in its continual revolution, raises up one man while another falls. A tragedy involved the descent of a great man (king or warrior or both) from most fortunate success to utter defeat and death. The suffering in these plays was often largely physical, and little depth of characterization was tried. But as Shakespeare grew up, the need was felt for a deeper, more subtle, and more flexible tragic form. Ideas from the ancient Greeks (Aristotle) and Romans (Seneca) were adopted, blended, insensibly altered: and the best fruits of this process are the major tragedies of Shakespeare. Of them, *Macbeth* is one of the clearest in its tragic pattern.

The object of the pattern is to gain the greatest possible response from the audience so that it may share fully in the tragic emotions of pity or sympathy, and fear or horror. These responses are gained first through our fellow-feeling for the sufferings of others, then through our deepest convictions as to right and wrong, our beliefs as to religion and the supernatural, and our repugnance at ugliness and discord. You will see as we define it, the means by which the pattern provides for the desired response.

The tragic hero must be a man great and admirable in both his powers and his opportunities. He should be a person so placed in society that his actions involve the well-being of all of its members.

The plot of the play should show him working to achieve some goal very dear to him. This action will involve him in choices. His downfall must be the result of a web of circumstances spun out of these choices which set off a train of events he did not or could not foresee, and which cannot be halted. He is thus caught. The hostility of his destiny may be a result of circumstances, of the activities of his enemies, or (and this is usual) some supernatural force hostile to him personally or to all humanity such as malevolent fate, the gods, Satan. When it is too late to escape, the victim

The Crowning of Macbeth

comes to realize what has happened to him, and dies finally, bitter, burnt-out, and desperate. The audience generally is acquainted with more of the action than the hero, and thus sees his evil destiny at work long before he does. This sets up an ironical tension, and is a powerful instrument for gaining the sympathy of the audience. The hero's death at the end very often, as in *Macbeth,* not only releases him from life's burden, and the audience from its tension, but also releases the hero's society from the disorder his downfall had caused.

IRONY AND
DRAMATIC IRONY

Irony is a special use of double meaning, as when someone makes a remark which while clearly saying one thing hints at a further and different meaning which only certain hearers would understand. The effect of such speech is often bitter and sinister, always concentrated and full of suggestion. Irony may be of situation as well as speech, as when Macbeth takes comfort from the prophecies about Birnham Wood and the man not born of woman. The speeches of Lennox in III, vi are full of conscious irony. The device is very effective in a tragedy like *Macbeth* because of the note of grim humor, the sharp twist, it can administer.

Dramatic irony is a special type. It depends on the fact that some characters know more than others, and that the audience can

see more than any of them. Thus quite innocent remarks will not have an innocent meaning to the audience. An example of this is Banquo's answer to Macbeth, who has just invited him to the banquet. Macbeth says, "Fail not our feast." And Banquo answers, "My lord, I will not."

SYMBOLISM

Macbeth's constant and most formidable enemies are supernatural, a fact which contributes to the intense tone of the play. They never rest; they or their agents, or nature disturbed and disordered by them, are constantly playing around the fringes of the action. We are kept aware of these sinister presences in part by a poetic use of symbols: symbols for good and evil, order and disorder, virtue, and vice. As the play develops they form a pattern so that the recurrence of one of them stirs an echo. They are noticed as they occur, but the following list gathers together some of the more obvious ones.

Evil
Hell
Disorder
Darkness
Good
Heaven
Order
Light

13

MACBETH

Dramatis Personae

DUNCAN, King of Scotland.

MALCOLM,
DONALBAIN, } his Sons.

MACBETH,
BANQUO, } Generals of the King's Army.

MACDUFF,
LENNOX,
ROSS,
MENTEITH, } Noblemen of Scotland.
ANGUS,
CAITHNESS,

FLEANCE, Son to Banquo.

SIWARD, Earl of Northumberland, General of the English
Forces.

YOUNG SIWARD, his Son.

SEYTON, an Officer attending Macbeth.

Boy, Son to Macduff.

An English Doctor.

A Scotch Doctor.

A Sergeant.

A Porter.

An Old Man.

LADY MACBETH.

LADY MACDUFF.

Gentlewoman attending on Lady Macbeth.

HECATE and Three Witches.

Lords, Gentlemen, Officers, Soldiers, Murderers, Attendants,
and Messengers. The Ghost of Banquo, and other Apparitions.

SCENE.—*Scotland, England.*

DUNCAN

PORTER

LADY MACBETH

FLEANCE

BANQUO

LADY MACDUFF

14

MACBETH

ACT I SCENE I

The dramatic purpose of the scene is to establish the theme of Satanic hideousness and disorder so fundamental to the play in a manner as striking as possible to the senses of the audience.

To appreciate the full force the scene had for its first audiences, we must first visualize the three hags as ugly as senility, poverty, disease, and malice can make them, out in a thunderstorm cackling greedily over their evil plans. Then we must realize that most of the watchers believed in witches, and their support by a real devil. They had all seen witches in the streets. Witches were often tried in the law courts, confessed, and were executed. Even the sceptics, and there were some, were unsure in their disbelief.

The following description of a witch was written by a sceptical writer (Bishop Bancroft) in 1603-5. A witch, he says, is "an old weather-beaten crone, having her chin and her knees meeting for age, walking like a bow leaning' on a shaft, hollow-eyed, untoothed, furrowed on her face, having her lips trembling with the palsy, going mumbling in the streets."

And here (by Gifford in 1597) is a standard account of the activity of witches, "that worketh by the devil, or by some devilish or curious art, either hurting or healing, revealing things secret, or foretelling things to come, which the devil hath devised to entangle and snare men's souls withal to damnation."

Thus the witches unite ugliness, evil, and power, in the service of disorder. And they seek Macbeth.

ACT I SCENE II

The alarm (drums) introduces us to a bright martial scene, the keynote of which is heroism. The regal costume of Duncan, his sons, and the other lords would be colorful and magnificent to suit with the full-throated grandiloquence of the sergeant's speech. The note of violent realism is injected by the sergeant's wounds. Blood was both plentiful and lifelike on the Jacobean stage.

Duncan and his soldiers embody virtue seeking order, and through Macbeth's victories, good order is restored. This is the happy state ruled by a gracious king (see I,vii,16-18; III,i,66; IV,iii,109.) that the witches would like to destroy; and Macbeth whom they will meet, is its most glorious hero.

Besides presenting the above picture, the scene introduces some important characters. Finally, in its

---

ACT ONE, scene one.

(A DESERT HEATH)

Thunder and lightning. Enter three Witches.

First Witch. When shall we three meet again   1
In thunder, lightning, or in rain?
Second Witch. When the Hurlyburly's done,   3
When the battle's lost and won.
Third Witch. That will be ere the set of sun.
First Witch. Where the place?
Second Witch.   Upon the heath.   6
Third Witch. There to meet with Macbeth.
First Witch. I come, Graymalkin!   8
Second Witch. Paddock calls.   9
Third Witch. Anon.
All. Fair is foul, and foul is fair: 11
Hover through the fog and filthy air.   [*Exeunt.*

Scene two.

(A CAMP NEAR FORRES)

Alarum within. Enter KING DUNCAN, MALCOLM, DONALBAIN, LENNOX *with* Attendants, *meeting a bleeding* Sergeant.

Duncan. What bloody man is that? He can report,   1
As seemeth by his plight, of the revolt
The newest state.
Malcolm.   This is the sergeant   3
Who, like a good and hardy soldier, fought   4
'Gainst my captivity. Hail, brave friend!   5
Say to the king the knowledge of the broil
As thou didst leave it.
Sergeant.   Doubtful it stood;
As two spent swimmers, that do cling together   8
And choke their art. The merciless Macdonwald—   9
Worthy to be a rebel, for to that   10
The multiplying villanies of nature   11
Do swarm upon him—from the western isles   12
Of kerns and gallowglasses is supplied;   13
And fortune, on his damned quarrel smiling,   14
Show'd like a rebel's whore: but all's too weak;   15
For brave Macbeth,—well he deserves that name,—
Disdaining fortune, with his brandish'd steel,
Which smok'd with bloody execution,
Like valour's minion carv'd out his passage   19
Till he fac'd the slave;   20
Which ne'er shook hands. nor bade farewell to him,   21
Till he unseam'd him from the nave to the chaps,   22
And fix'd his head upon our battlements.
Duncan. O valiant cousin! worthy gentleman!   24

MACBETH

ACT I SCENE II

closing lines, Macbeth is suitably rewarded for his service, and a second meeting is provided for, as Duncan sends Ross to greet him with the news. By this device Macbeth is made the center toward which both the king's and the witches's desires converge.

CHARACTERS: Seen through the eyes of others, Macbeth seems powerful and fortunate, a nature admired and loved (see lines 16, 55) by his comrades.

Duncan is an old man (see V,i,37), but there is no reason to think him doddering (as some actors have represented him). Look at the ages of his sons; Malcolm, the elder, to judge from his actions, can scarcely be out of his teens. ("What's the boy Malcolm" [V,iii,3]). Neither is it necessary to charge him with cowardice for not being in the thick of the fight, any more than with a modern army general. "A camp near Forres," the stage direction says; but it was added to the play in 1709, in Nicholas Rowe's edition. Both the alarm and the sergeant's still bleeding wounds indicate how close Duncan must be to the actual fighting. In performance Duncan and his companions march onto the stage "meeting a bloody sergeant." If the sergeant is coming from the battle, the King must be going towards it. The chief unmistakable trait of character Duncan shows is a quick enthusiasm in expressing his pleasure, and praising his supporters.

SOURCES AND HISTORICAL POINTS: The events reported here are taken from Holinshed's CHRONICLES. The only notable detail not therefrom is the precise mention of the sum of 10,000 dollars which Sweno is supposed to have paid (see below). Now when King Christian IV of Denmark, brother of James I's wife, came to visit her and her husband in 1606, he gave exactly 10,000 dollars to King James's officers to be distributed as largess to the servants of the household. Shakespeare's actors were among these servants, and will have received a share of this gift. They performed often for the two monarchs at this time, and there is some likelihood that MACBETH was one of the plays so given.

The Norse invasion used by Shakespeare was led by Canute to avenge the earlier defeat of Sweno. Holinshed says, "They that escaped and got once to their ships, obtained of Macbeth FOR A GREAT SUM OF GOLD, that such of their friends as were slain at this last bickering might be buried in Saint Colme's Inch."

Sergeant. As whence the sun 'gins his reflection   25
Shipwracking storms and direful thunders break,
So from that spring whence comfort seem'd to come
Discomfort swells. Mark, King of Scotland, mark:
No sooner justice had with valour arm'd
Compell'd these skipping kerns to trust their heels,
But the Norweyan lord, surveying vantage,   31
With furbish'd arms and new supplies of men   32
Began a fresh assault.
   Duncan.   Dismay'd not this
Our captains, Macbeth and Banquo?
   Sergeant.   Yes;   34
As sparrows eagles, or the hare the lion.
If I say sooth, I must report they were   36
As cannons overcharg'd with double cracks; So they   37

Doubly redoubled strokes upon the foe:
Except they meant to bathe in reeking wounds,   40
Or memorize another Golgotha,   41
I cannot tell—   42
But I am faint, my gashes cry for help.
   Duncan. So well thy words become thee as thy
     wounds;
They smack of honour both. Go, get him surgeons.
                [*Exeunt* SERGEANT, *attended.*

                Enter ROSS.

Who comes here?
   Malcolm.   The worthy Thane of Ross.   46
   Lennox. What a haste looks through his eyes! So   47
     should he look
That seems to speak things strange.   48
   Ross.   God save the king!
   Duncan. Whence cam'st thou, worthy thane?
   Ross.   From Fife, great king;
Where the Norweyan banners flout the sky   50
And fan our people cold. Norway himself,
With terrible numbers,
Assisted by that most disloyal traitor,
The Thane of Cawdor, began a dismal conflict;   54
Till that Bellona's bridegroom, lapp'd in proof,
Confronted him with self-comparisons,   56
Point against point, rebellious arm 'gainst arm,
Curbing his lavish spirit: and, to conclude,   58
The victory fell on us.—
   Duncan.   Great happiness!
   Ross. That now   60
Sweno, the Norways' king, craves composition;   61
Nor would we deign him burial of his men
Till he disbursed, at Saint Colme's Inch,   63
Ten thousand dollars to our general use.
   Duncan. No more that Thane of Cawdor shall
     deceive
Our bosom interest. Go pronounce his present
     death,
And with his former title greet Macbeth.
   Ross. I'll see it done.
   Duncan. What he hath lost noble Macbeth hath
     won.
                   [*Exeunt.*

25-28. "whence...swells": the sun rises in the east, but so do storms. Likewise the bad news of the Norwegian king's invasion after a victory over Macdonwald.

25. "reflection": return.

31. "Norweyan": Norwegian, i.e., Sweno, king of Norway.

31. "vantage": advantage.

32. "furbish'd": freshly polished implying that they hadn't been in battle yet.

34. "Yes": ironical, as the following line shows.

36. "sooth": truth.

37. "cracks": charges. (Cannons were used in Shakespeare's day but not in Macbeth's. This is an anachronism.)

40. "Except": unless.

41. "memorize...Golgotha": make this battlefield as famous as Golgotha.

42. "I cannot tell": he becomes faint here and doesn't finish the sentence. He was probably going to say: I cannot tell what their purpose was.

46. "Thane": an old title of nobility in Scotland almost equal to that of earl.

47. "What...eyes!": what an expression of haste there is in his eyes!

48. "seems to speak": looks as if he were about to speak.

50. "flout": mock.

51. "fan . . . cold": their banners now serve merely to cool off our victorious soldiers.

54. "dismal": threatening disaster.

55. "Bellona's bridegroom": Macbeth. Bellona was the Roman goddess of war.

"lapp'd in proof": clad in well-tested armor.

56. "Confronted . . . comparisons": met him in single combat and made him compare himself with Macbeth.

57. "Point . . . point": sword against sword.

58. "lavish": insolent.

60. "that": so that.

61. "craves composition": begs for terms of peace.

63. "Inch": Celtic for island.

64. "dollars": these Danish silver coins were first minted in 1518. (See commentary.)

16

MACBETH

ACT I SCENE II

Line 65 gains ironical significance in view of what follows. Ironies of this kind, that look forward, are effective in performance beginning with the second viewing of the play, or from the first when the main outline of the story is known in advance, which is often the case especially in historical plays.

ACT I SCENE III

Place name was added in 1709, but Shakespeare specified this one. (See I,i,6; I,iii,77). It is symbolically right, for it suggests a waste place subject to nature's laws, but itself formless, unproductive, deserted.

Circumstantial accounts of witchcraft were written by King James in both DAEMONOLOGIE and NEWS FROM SCOTLAND, some of which apply to the witches's scenes, e.g.:

Agnis Tompson's testimony at her trial (News from Scotland): "In the night a cat was conveyed into the midst of the sea by all these witches SAILING IN THEIR RIDDLES OR SIEVES, and left right before the town of Lieth in Scotland: this done, there did arise such a tempest in the sea, as a greater has not been seen. . . . Again it is confessed, that the said cat was the cause that the King's Majesty's ship at his coming forth of Denmark had a contrary wind to the rest of his ships, then being in his company, which thing was most strange and true, as the King's Majesty acknowledged, for when the rest of the ships had a fair and good wind, then was the wind contrary and altogether against his Majesty's, and further the said witch declared that his Majesty had never come safely from the sea if his faith had not prevailed above their intentions." (This establishes a pattern for viewing the trials of Macbeth and Banquo: faith alone can prevail above their intentions.)

From DAEMONOLOGIE: "They can raise storms and tempests in the air either upon sea or land, though not universally, but in such prescribed bounds as God will permit them." (One of Satan's titles is Prince of the Air.)

With respect to the sailor and his wife, the witches betray the motives King James ascribed to them, revenge and greed caused by poverty.

Rituals such as this formal dance figure were their methods of calling upon their master.

Scene three.

(A HEATH)

Thunder. Enter the three Witches.

First Witch. Where hast thou been, sister?
Second Witch. Killing swine.
Third Witch. Sister, where thou?
First Witch. A sailor's wife had chestnuts in her lap,
And munch'd, and munch'd, and munch'd: 'Give me,' quoth I:
'Aroint thee, witch!' the rump-fed ronyon cries.   6
Her husband's to Aleppo gone, master o' the Tiger: 7
But in a sieve I'll thither sail,
And, like a rat without a tail,   9
I'll do, I'll do, and I'll do.   10
Second Witch. I'll give thee a wind.   11
First Witch. Thou'rt kind.
Third Witch. And I another.
First Witch. I myself have all the other;   14
And the very ports they blow,   15
All the quarters that they know
I' the shipman's card.   17
I'll drain him dry as hay: 18
Sleep shall neither night nor day
Hang upon his pent-house lid;   20
He shall live a man forbid.   21
Weary se'nnights nine times nine   22
Shall he dwindle, peak and pine: 23
Though his bark cannot be lost,   24
Yet it shall be tempest-tost.
Look what I have.
Second Witch. Show me, show me.
First Witch. Here I have a pilot's thumb,   28
Wrack'd as homeward he did come.   [*Drum within.*
Third Witch. A drum! a drum!
Macbeth doth come.
All. The weird sisters, hand in hand,   32
Posters of the sea and land,   33
Thus do go about, about:
Thrice to thine, and thrice to mine,   35
And thrice again, to make up nine.
Peace! the charm's wound up.

Enter MACBETH *and* BANQUO.

Macbeth. So foul and fair a day I have not seen.   38
Banquo. How far is 't call'd to Forres? What are these,   39
So wither'd and so wild in their attire,
That look not like th' inhabitants o' the earth,
And yet are on 't? Live you? or are you aught   42
That man may question? You seem to understand me,   43
By each at once her choppy finger laying   44
Upon her skinny lips: you should be women,
And yet your beards forbid me to interpret
That you are so.

17

---

6. "rump-fed": fed with expensive cuts of meat.

6. "ronyon": a term of abuse or contempt.

7. "Aleppo": in Syria (Asia Minor).

7. "Tiger": a common name, for a ship in Shakespeare's time.

9. "without a tail": witches, according to the belief, could assume the shape of animals; but because they were creatures of Satan, they were not made perfect and thus lacked tails.

10. "I'll do": she will work mischief on the ship and extend its journey.

11. "a wind": witches had control of the wind and weather.

14. "all the other": by subduing all the other winds and controlling one, she means to keep the Tiger tempest bound.

15. "ports they blow": by controlling the directions of the wind, she will keep the Tiger out to sea.

17. "card": compass face marking out the directions.

18. "drain him": by keeping the Tiger out, they will use up their supply of water and thus be exhausted from thirst.

20. "pent-house lid": the eyelid that resembles a sloped roof.

21. "forbid": to put under a spell or curse.

22. "se'nnights": a week.

23. "dwindle, peak, and pine": literally, to grow thin, waste away.

24. "cannot be lost": it shall come into harbor anyway.

28. "thumb": parts of dead bodies were used to aid the witchcraft.

32. "weird sisters": Weird, meant fateful. In Holinshed it was said that the three women in antique dress who met Macbeth and Banquo in the wood were the three fates of Graeco-Roman mythology. Shakespeare, while changing them from goddesses into witches, has retained the above title for them. They are called witches in the play, only by the "rump-fed ronyon." The emphasis on their connection with fate has the effect of making them seem more serious and important than ordinary witches. Their precise identity is left vague.

33. "posters-land" swift travelers, the witches could travel over the land swiftly.

35. "thrice to thine . . . to mine": rotating three times in your direction and three times in mine. This was supposed to complete the charm.

38. "foul and fair": foul because of the weather; fair because of the victory.

39. "Forres": the Scottish capital, near Inverness.

42. "are on't": part of it, belong to it.

43. "question": talk to.

44. "choppy": chopped, cracked.

MACBETH

ACT I SCENE III

The scene marks the culmination of the play so far, in the two meetings prepared by the first two scenes. Macbeth has reached a plateau in his life. The war is over; he has risen as far as he can reasonably expect to, and now inactivity would seem like subsiding. The meetings put him successively in touch with the two worlds in which he and his action will live, the supernatural/evil and the human/virtuous (though not purely so). Banquo to his lesser degree is in a similar position. With these meetings, and Macbeth's reaction to them, begins the tragic action.

Macbeth's first speech ironically echoes the witches's "Fair is foul and foul is fair." It points up the symbolism too by reminding us of the disordered elements.

Their second greeting provides a case of dramatic irony because we have heard Duncan's words (I,ii,66) and can see the subtlety of their trap.

Macbeth's silence illustrates how close their greeting has come to his secret wishes. King James's words are again to the point: "That old and crafty enemy of ours assails none, except he first find an entresse ready for him." (DAEMONOLOGIE).

Public attention was called to Holinshed's account of the prophecy to Banquo and Macbeth as a result of the reception staged for the King by the students of St. John's College, Oxford, during his visit in 1605. "Three young youths in habit and attire like nymphs or sybils, confronted the King, saluting him and putting him in mind of that ancient prophecy made unto Banquo, his Majesty's ancestor...." It is supposed by some that this famous incident may have sent Shakespeare to his Holinshed looking for a subject.

The witches will have vanished through the aid of a trapdoor in the stage.

The marked difference in Macbeth and Banquo's feelings about the witches provides an index to their characters. Imaginative Macbeth marvels at their "melting"; Banquo treats them with rational doubt and a trace of casualness.

Things are happening too swiftly. Throughout the rest of the act the effect is of events crowding Macbeth's judgment.

Macbeth. Speak, if you can: what are you?

First Witch. All hail, Macbeth! hail to thee, Thane of Glamis!

Second Witch. All hail, Macbeth! hail to thee, Thane of Cawdor!   48

Third Witch. All hail, Macbeth! that shalt be king hereafter.   49

Banquo. Good sir, why do you start, and seem to fear

Things that do sound so fair? I' the name of truth,

Are ye fantastical, or that indeed   53

Which outwardly ye show? My noble partner   54

You greet with present grace and great prediction

Of noble having and of royal hope,   56

That he seems rapt withal: to me you speak not.   57

If you can look into the seeds of time,   58

And say which grain will grow and which will not,

Speak then to me, who neither beg nor fear

Your favours nor your hate.

First Witch. Hail!

Second Witch. Hail!

Third Witch. Hail!

First Witch. Lesser than Macbeth, and greater.

Second Witch. Not so happy, yet much happier.

Third Witch. Thou shalt get kings, though thou be none: 67

So, all hail, Macbeth and Banquo!

First Witch. Banquo and Macbeth, all hail!

Macbeth. Stay, you imperfect speakers, tell me more: 70

By Sinel's death I know I am Thane of Glamis;   71

But how of Cawdor? the Thane of Cawdor lives,

A prosperous gentleman; and to be king

Stands not within the prospect of belief,   74

No more than to be Cawdor. Say from whence   75

You owe this strange intelligence? or why   76

Upon this blasted heath you stop our way   77

With such prophetic greeting? Speak, I charge you.

                         [*Witches vanish.*

Banquo. The earth hath bubbles as the water has,

And these are of them. Whither are they vanish'd?   80

Macbeth. Into the air, and what seem'd corporal melted   81

As breath into the wind. Would they had stay'd!

Banquo. Were such things here as we do speak about?

Or have we eaten on the insane root   84

That takes the reason prisoner?

Macbeth. Your children shall be kings.

Banquo.   You shall be king.

Macbeth. And Thane of Cawdor too; went it not so?

Banquo. To the self-same tune and words. Who's here?

Enter ROSS and ANGUS

Ross. The king hath happily receiv'd, Macbeth,

The news of thy success; and when he reads

Thy personal venture in the rebels' fight,

His wonders and his praises do contend   92

Which should be thine or his. Silenc'd with that,   93

---

48. "Glamis": an Eastern Scottish village.

49. "Cawdor": a small village near Inverness. Titles are usually attached to some section of the country.

53. "fantastical": imaginary creations; of the fancy.

54. "show": appear to be.

56. "noble having": this refers to the prophecy of the witches that Macbeth will become Thane of Cawdor.

57. "withal": by it, therewith.

58. "seeds": future events that might or might not occur.

67. "get": beget, propagate.

70. "imperfect": obscure.

71. "Sinel": Macbeth's father.

74. "the prospect of belief": the greatest distance the mind will venture into the future on what it believes.

75-76. "from whence-intelligence": from what place did you get this information.

76. "owe": have, possess.

77. "blasted": barren.

80. "are of them": belong to that category.

81. "corporal": material.

84. "insane root": probably either hemlock or henbane.

92-3. "his wonders and his": contest between dumb wonder and the desires to express his praise.

93. "with that": by that mental struggle.

MACBETH

ACT I SCENE III

From this moment both Macbeth and Banquo take the prophecies more seriously, but notice that Banquo's judgment is at once from a religious viewpoint: if the witches were serious they represent the devil, and lead to harm. It might be his descendant, James I, speaking.

The scene provides a good example of Shakespeare's improvement on history. Both the words and the circumstances of their meeting with the weird sisters are taken almost unchanged from Holinshed (though he had called them goddesses of destiny), but in the chronicle a long time passes before Cawdor's treason is discovered and his title given to Macbeth.

The importance of this aside cannot be overstated. It shows us the nature of Macbeth's ambition (i.e., for imperial power), the way in which his vivid imagination controls his thought and can seem the prime reality, and how the prophecy has already caused division (i.e., disorder) in his mind (see note).

Macbeth's seeming triumph over temptation is a truce rather than a victory. He has not outlawed his desire.

Banquo's echo of lines 108-9 ("borrow'd robes") emphasizes this image. Keep your eyes on it; it returns.

In viewing o'er the rest o' the self-same day,
He finds thee in the stout Norweyan ranks,
Nothing afeard of what thyself didst make,
Strange images of death. As thick as hail   97
Came post with post, and every one did bear   98
Thy praises in his kingdom's great defence,
And pour'd them down before him.

Angus   We are sent
To give thee from our royal master thanks;
Only to herald thee into his sight,
Not pay thee.

Ross. And, for an earnest of a greater honour,   104
He bade me, from him, call thee Thane of Cawdor:
In which addition, hail, most worthy thane!   106
For it is thine.

Banquo.   What! can the devil speak true?

Macbeth. The Thane of Cawdor lives: why do you   108
    dress me
In borrow'd robes?

Angus.   Who was the thane lives yet;
But under heavy judgment bears that life
Which he deserves to lose. Whether he was   111
    combin'd
With those of Norway, or did line the rebel   112
With hidden help or vantage, or that with both   113
He labour'd in his country's wrack, I know not;
But treasons capital, confess'd and prov'd,   115
Have overthrown him.

Macbeth. [*Aside.*] Glamis, and Thane of Cawdor:
The greatest is behind. [*To* ROSS *and* ANGUS.]   117
    Thanks for your pains.
    [*To* BANQUO.] Do you not hope your children shall
    be kings,
When those that give the Thane of Cawdor to me
Promis'd no less to them?

Banquo.   That, trusted home,   120
Might yet enkindle you unto the crown,   121
Besides the Thane of Cawdor. But 'tis strange:
And oftentimes, to win us to our harm,
The instruments of darkness tell us truths,
Win us with honest trifles, to betray's   125
In deepest consequence.
Cousins, a word, I pray you.

Macbeth. [*Aside.*]   Two truths are told,
As happy prologues to the swelling act   128
Of the imperial theme. I thank you, gentlemen.
[*Aside.*] This supernatural soliciting   130
Cannot be ill, cannot be good; if ill,   131
Why hath it given me earnest of success,   132
Commencing in a truth? I am Thane of Cawdor:
If good, why do I yield to that suggestion   134
Whose horrid image doth unfix my hair
And make my seated heart knock at my ribs,   136
Against the use of nature? Present fears   137
Are less than horrible imaginings;
My thought, whose murder yet is but fantastical,   139
Shakes so my single state of man that function   140
Is smother'd in surmise, and nothing is   141
But what is not.

Banquo.   Look, how our partner's rapt.

97. "strange images of death": death takes on horrible and strange forms.

98. "post with post": relay system of messenger—(here it means post after post).

104. "earnest": down payment, pledge.

106. "in which addition": in acquiring another title.

108. "dress me": Shakespeare is remarkably fond of metaphors from clothing.

111. "combin'd": allied secretly.

112. "line the rebel": aided Macdonwald.

113. "hidden help": evidently he was not present in person.

115. "capital": meriting the death penalty.

117. "is behind": yet to follow.

120. "home": to the full.

121. "enkindle you": fire you with aspirations.

125. "win us": gain our confidence.

128. "prologues": the introduction to a play (usually a speech).

128. "swelling": stately.

130. "supernatural soliciting": the attempt of the witches to influence him into thinking he will be king.

131. "good": from a good source.

131. "ill": from an evil source.

132. "earnest": assurance, pledge.

134. "yield to that suggestion": the suggestion that he should murder Duncan.

136. "seated": not easily stirred up.

137. "against the use of nature?": contrary to my natural thoughts and actions.

137. "Present fears": hallucinations of fear.

139. "fantastical": imaginary.

140. "my single state of man": my single-minded state. After this experience he is, as it were, at war with himself: his better nature and his active self do not agree.

140. "function": the power to perform.

141. "surmise": conjecture or prophecy as to the future.

141-2. ". . . and nothing is But what is not." I am oblivious of the facts and can visualize nothing but the specters of my mind (i.e., the proposed murdering of Duncan).

MACBETH

ACT I SCENE III

ACT I SCENE IV

Just as the thunder of Scene Three recalled that of Scene One, the regal splendor here recalls Scene Two. Here the costumes will have a more festive air—court robes instead of military.

The scene is highly dramatic, full of irony, and contrasted emotions. Evil already disfigures the world's harmony.

There is no account of Cawdor in Holinshed. This picture of his gallant death may have been suggested by either or both of two famous traitors of the age, both of whom met their execution with gallant repentance, the Earl of Essex, and Sir Everard Digby, a favorite of James who had offered "hidden help and vantage" to the Gunpowder Plot in 1605. Whatever its source, the passage is highly effective. It breathes a kind of health as of virtue triumphant, and enables Duncan to make his unconsciously ironic and very characteristic reflection before greeting, with all his ready trust, the new Thane of Cawdor.

Macbeth's speech is extraordinarily stilted. Why?

Duncan here, and Ross later (IV, ii,28-9) give way to tears. This is not, to a citizen of the times, so much a sign of womanly weakness as it is of honest feeling. Men were expected then to be demonstrative, and a cold man was mistrusted. Our stiff-upper-lip ideal is of much later development.

King Kenneth, Duncan's great grandfather, had persuaded the

Macbeth. [*Aside.*] If chance will have me king, 143
why, chance may crown me,
Without my stir.
Banquo.   New honours come upon him,
Like our strange garments, cleave not to their mould 145
But with the aid of use.
Macbeth.   [*Aside.*] Come what come may, 146
Time and the hour runs through the roughest day. 147
Banquo. Worthy Macbeth, we stay upon your 148
leisure.
Macbeth. Give me your favour: my dull brain was 149
wrought
With things forgotten. Kind gentlemen, your pains
Are register'd where every day I turn 151
The leaf to read them. Let us toward the king.
Think upon what hath chanc'd; and, at more time,
The interim having weigh'd it, let us speak 154
Our free hearts each to other.
Banquo.   Very gladly.
Macbeth. Till then, enough. Come, friends.
                         [*Exeunt.*

Scene four.

(FORRES. A ROOM IN THE PALACE)

Flourish. Enter DUNCAN, MALCOLM, DONALBAIN, LENNOX, *and* Attendants.

Duncan. Is execution done on Cawdor? Are not
Those in commission yet return'd?
Malcolm   My liege, 2
They are not yet come back; but I have spoke
With one that saw him die; who did report
That very frankly he confess'd his treasons,
Implor'd your highness' pardon and set forth 6
A deep repentance. Nothing in his life
Became him like the leaving it; he died
As one that had been studied in his death 9
To throw away the dearest thing he ow'd, 10
As 'twere a careless trifle.
Duncan.   There's no art 11
To find the mind's construction in the face: 12
He was a gentleman on whom I built
An absolute trust.

Enter MACBETH, BANQUO, ROSS, *and* ANGUS.
          O worthiest cousin!
The sin of my ingratitude even now
Was heavy on me. Thou art so far before 16
That swiftest wing of recompense is slow
To overtake thee; would thou hadst less deserv'd, 18
That the proportion both of thanks and payment 19
Might have been mine! only I have left to say, 20
More is thy due than more than all can pay. 21
Macbeth. The service and the loyalty I owe,
In doing it, pays itself. Your highness, part 23

143-4. "If chance will . . . Without my stir": Macbeth as a member of the royal family is eligible for the crown as it is elective. He tries to supplant the thoughts of murder, with the thought that he will be elected.

145. "cleave not to their mould": the honors do not fit themselves comfortably to the wearer.

146. "use": habit, custom.

147. "Time . . . day": hour by hour even the longest day comes to an end. I'll let things go as they will and await the outcome.

148. "stay upon your leisure": we await your action.

149. "wrought": disturbed.

151. "regist'red": kept within my mind.

154. "The interim having weigh'd it": when we have thought it over in the meantime.

2. "Those in commission": the royal commissioners appointed to attend to Cawdor's trial and execution.

6. "Implor'd": begged.
"set forth": showed, revealed.

9-11. "had been . . . trifle": had learned the lesson how, at death, to part with his dearest possession (life) easily.

9. "studied": i.e., as one who had rehearsed the act of meeting death.

10. "ow'd": owned, possessed.

11. "As": as if.

11. "careless": uncared for, worthless, insignificant.

11-12. It is impossible to tell the character of a man's thoughts from the expression on his face.

12. "construction": meaning.

16. "Thou": Duncan uses the familiar and affectionate "thou" instead of the more formal "you" in speaking to his nearest kinsman.

18-20. I wish that you had deserved less, so that the reward I give you might have been more instead of less than your deserts.

19. "the proportion": the larger proportion, the right proportion, the due relation.

20. "mine": on my side of the account: so that the balance might stand in my favor (as having paid more than I owed)—in my power to render.

21. "More is thy due": more than all I can do is due to you.

23. "pays itself": is its own reward.

MACBETH

ACT I SCENE IV

thanes to agree to a law providing for hereditary succession to the throne as follows: "The eldest male heir of the king should succeed regardless of age: the nephew by a son is preferred over a nephew by a daughter, a brother's son before a sister's, etc." But Kenneth's son did not succeed. He had to wait until the usurper Grime was dislodged before he was crowned Malcolm II. He again urged his father's law on the reluctant thanes. Since Malcolm II had only daughters, the next king was to be one of his grandsons, Duncan or Macbeth. (Holinshed's Duncan is younger than Macbeth. Shakespeare may have reversed the ages in the play in order to provide Duncan with a clearer hereditary title to the throne.) and Duncan was chosen. Since the thanes favored the older system, under which Macbeth might hope for election, Duncan's naming Malcolm Prince of Cumberland (i.e. heir to the throne) is dramatic.

Here is the first eloquent call for darkness to hide evil deeds. Black (along with red) is Satan's color.

ACT I SCENE V

This dark and powerful scene needs little commentary, except as to the riddle of Lady Macbeth's character. She is inflamed by the idea of Macbeth crowned, but what makes her drive so headlong into evil? She does not deliberate an instant, and here may be a clue. She has a quick practical intelligence (see II,ii and III,iv) that leaves out of its calculations her deeply passionate nature. She seems to live in the present and for the future. "What's done is done" (III,ii,12) she rightly says; then, she wrongly assumes that it is also done with.

Is to receive our duties; and our duties 24
Are to your throne and state, children and servants;
Which do but what they should, by doing everthing
Safe toward your love and honour.
Duncan. Welcome hither: 27
I have begun to plant thee, and will labour 28
To make thee full of growing. Noble Banquo,
That hast no less deserv'd, nor must be known
No less to have done so, let me infold thee
And hold thee to my heart.
Banquo. There if I grow,
The harvest is your own.
Duncan. My plenteous joys 33
Wanton in fulness, seek to hide themselves 34
In drops of sorrow. Sons, kinsmen, thanes, 35
And you whose places are the nearest, know
We will establish our estate upon 37
Our eldest, Malcolm, whom we name hereafter
The Prince of Cumberland; which honour must
Not unaccompanied invest him only,
But signs of nobleness, like stars, shall shine 41
On all deservers. From hence to Inverness, 42
And bind us further to you. 43
Macbeth. The rest is labour, which is not us'd for 44
you:
I'll be myself the harbinger, and make joyful 45
The hearing of my wife with your approach;
So, humbly take my leave.
Duncan. My worthy Cawdor!
Macbeth. [*Aside.*] The Prince of Cumberland!
that is a step 48
On which I must fall down, or else o'er-leap,
For in my way it lies. Stars, hide your fires!
Let not light see my black and deep desires;
The eye wink at the hand; yet let that be 52
Which the eye fears, when it is done, to see. [*Exit.*
Duncan. True, worthy Banquo; he is full so
valiant, 54
And in his commendations I am fed;
It is a banquet to me. Let's after him,
Whose care is gone before to bid us welcome:
It is a peerless kinsman. [*Flourish. Exeunt.*

Scene five.

(INVERNESS. MACBETH'S CASTLE)
Enter LADY MACBETH, *reading a letter.*

*They met me in the day of success; and I have
learned by the perfectest report, they have more* 2
in them than mortal knowledge. When I burned in 3
*desire to question them further, they made themselves
air, into which they vanished. Whiles I
stood rapt in the wonder of it, came missives* 6
*from the king, who all-hailed me, 'Thane of Cawdor;'
by which title, before, these weird sisters
saluted me, and referred me to the coming on of* 9
time, with, 'Hail, king that shalt be!' This have I 10

24-25. Our duties are servant and children to your throne and state. It is our duty to serve you.

26-27. "everything . . . honor": everything that tends to safeguard and fulfill our obligation to love and honour you.

27. "Safe toward": so as not to fail in the love and honor that is due to you.

28. "to plant thee": i.e., by making thee Thane of Cawdor.

33. If I take root when you press me to your heart, and grow there like a tree, whatever fruit I bear shall be yours.

34. "Wanton": unrestrained, perverse, contrary.

35. "drops of sorrow": tears.

37. "We will": it is our royal purpose. "establish our estate upon": settle the succession of the throne on, name as our successor.

41. There is a general distribution of honors when the Prince is formally invested with his new title.

42. "From hence": let us go hence. "Inverness": where Macbeth's castle is.

43. "bind us further": lay us under further obligations, as our host; oblige me still further by receiving me as a guest.

44. Our leisure time is wearisome if it is not spent in your service.

45. "harbinger": an officer sent ahead (when a king intends to visit a place) to arrange for proper lodgings for him and his suite.

48. "a step": an advance in honor (for Malcolm).

52. "The eye wink at the hand": let my eyes not see the deed that my hand commits; be blind to its deeds.

54-55. Banquo had every reason to be jealous of Macbeth; but he is generous enough to add his commendations to Duncan's praise of his rival.

2. "report": intelligence, information.

3. "mortal": human.

6. "missives": usually letters; here, messengers.

9-10. "the coming on of time": future.

MACBETH

ACT I SCENE V

Her analysis of Macbeth's character is admirable evidence of her understanding and its limitations; she cannot read Macbeth's positive loathing or evil, a feeling that cannot quite be described as either virtue or fear.

The breathlessness of the messenger underlines the swift pace of events mentioned above (I,iii).

Here (lines 30 and 37) is the joyful "hearing" of I,iv,45-6.

The raven is intended as a metaphor for the hoarse messenger, but lives as a symbol in its own right, the black, ugly, carrion crow.

This famous speech is in the form of a prayer asking the evil spirits to make her monstrous. It ends with the second of the play's invocations to darkness (cf. "Stars hide your fires . . . I,iv,50-3).

thought good to deliver thee, my dearest partner 11
of greatness, that thou mightest not lose the dues 12
of rejoicing, but being ignorant of what greatness 13
is promised thee. Lay it to thy heart, and fare- 13a
well.
Glamis thou art, and Cawdor; and shalt be 14
What thou art promis'd. Yet do I fear thy nature; 15
It is too full o' the milk of human kindness
To catch the nearest way; thou wouldst be great, 17
Art not without ambition, but without
The illness should attend it; what thou wouldst 19
    highly,
That thou wouldst holily; wouldst not play false,
And yet wouldst wrongly win; thou'dst have, great
    Glamis,
That which cries, 'Thus thou must do, if thou have it;'
And that which rather thou dost fear to do
Than wishest should be undone. Hie thee hither, 24
That I may pour my spirits in thine ear, 25
And chastise with the valour of my tongue 26
All that impedes thee from the golden round, 27
Which fate and metaphysical aid doth seem 28
To have thee crown'd withal.

Enter a Messenger.

　　　　　　　　What is your tidings?
Messenger. The king comes here to-night.
Lady Macbeth. 　　　　　Thou'rt mad to say it.
Is not thy master with him? who, were't so,
Would have inform'd for preparation.
Messenger. So please you, it is true: our thane is
    coming;
One of my fellows had the speed of him, 34
Who, almost dead for breath, had scarcely more
Than would make up his message.
Lady Macbeth. 　　　　　Give him tending;
He brings great news.—[*Exit* Messenger.] The raven 37
    himself is hoarse
That croaks the fatal entrance of Duncan
Under my battlements. Come, you spirits
That tend on mortal thoughts! unsex me here, 40
And fill me from the crown to the toe top full
Of direst cruelty; make thick my blood, 42
Stop up the access and passage to remorse, 43
That no compunctious visitings of nature 44
Shake my fell purpose, nor keep peace between 45
The effect and it! Come to my woman's breasts,
And take my milk for gall, you murdering ministers, 47
Wherever in your sightless substances 48
You wait on nature's mischief! Come, thick night, 49
And pall thee in the dunnest smoke of hell, 50
That my keen knife see not the wound it makes, 51
Nor heaven peep through the blanket of the dark,
To cry, 'Hold, hold!'

Enter MACBETH

　　　　Great Glamis! worthy Cawdor!
Greater than both, by the all-hail hereafter! 54
Thy letters have transported me beyond 55
This ignorant present, and I feel now 56
The future in the instant.

11-12. "partner of greatness": Macbeth and his wife are so deeply attached to each other that neither can think of any division or individuality in their interest.

12-13. "the dues of rejoicing": the opportunity to rejoice which is due to you.

15. "fear": fear for, i.e., fear the weakness of.

17. "the nearest way": meaning murder.

19. "illness": evil, ill qualities.

24. "Hie": hasten.

25. "my spirits": my resolutions and energy of will.

26. "chastise": drive away all the scruples and fears which may keep you from gaining the crown; rebuke, suppress.

27. "All that impedes thee": i.e., your fear, gentleness of nature and scruples of conscience.
"the golden round": sovereignty, the crown.

28. "metaphysical": supernatural.

28-9. "seem . . . withal": seem to intend to cause thee to be crowned with.

34. "had the speed of him": made better speed than he.

37. "The raven": the croaking of the raven was supposed to forbode death. Perhaps Lady Macbeth refers to the hoarse voice of the messenger.

40. "mortal": murderous, deadly.

42. "make thick my blood": blood thickened by melancholy was thought to cause gloomy ferocity of disposition.

43. "the access . . . remorse": every way of approach by which regret can reach my heart.

44. "compunctious . . . nature": natural instincts of compassion.

45. "fell": cruel, savage.

47. "murdering ministers": are the "spirits that tend on mortal thoughts."

48. "sightless": invisible.

49. "nature's mischief": the evil things in our nature.

50. "dunnest": darkest.

51. "my keen knife": Lady Macbeth thinks of the deed as her own.

54. "the all-hail hereafter": she speaks as if she actually heard the witches.

55. "transported me": carried me forward as a vision.

56. "ignorant": ignorant because unaware of what the future will bring.

MACBETH

ACT I SCENE V

Macbeth seems anxious not to commit himself; these short lines speak volumes as to the turmoil in his mind. But note that the actor can alter the interpretation of his character at this point by his pronunciation of line 59. Alec Guiness (The Old Vic on RCA records) states it without irony, as if stating a fact in answer to a question whose irony he rejects.

Macbeth has apparently the virtuous man's habit of letting his face express his feelings, just as Duncan has the virtuous man's habit of judging a man by his face. This trait in Macbeth is one of many that unfit him for perfect villainy, and facilitate our sympathy.

ACT I SCENE VI

This light and socially gracious scene derives its ironic and symbolic power from the echoes of Scene Five still ringing in our ears. Since Lady Macbeth's reference to "my battlements" (I,v,39), we view the castle as a sort of man trap baited for the unsuspecting Duncan. The castle, since it is controlled by Lady Macbeth, is a place of evil. Its walls, then, are the boundaries between good and evil. The opening speeches give symbolic expression to the serenity and order still reigning on the outside. The supernatural source of the opposition is again implicit here in Banquo's lines (4 and 5). If it is heaven's breath outside, what must it be within? The temple-haunting martlet is balanced also against Lady Macbeth's raven.

Notice how Lady Macbeth's first speech, flowing oilily on for four lines with only the lightest pauses, gains from its rhythm the air of premeditated hypocrisy.

The word "love" occurs five times in the scene in various senses: love of subjects for their monarch (l.11), of husband for wife (l.23), of monarch for his loyal subjects (l.29).

Picture the action on stage as the last line of the scene is spoken and Duncan passes under the battlements. With what gesture will Lady Macbeth take Duncan's arm?

Macbeth.   My dearest love,   57
Duncan comes here to-night.
Lady Macbeth.   And when goes hence?
Macbeth. To-morrow, as he purposes.
Lady Macbeth.   O! never
Shall sun that morrow see.
Your face, my thane, is as a book where men
May read strange matters. To beguile the time,   62
Look like the time; bear welcome in your eye,
Your hand, your tongue: look like the innocent
     flower,
But be the serpent under 't. He that's coming
Must be provided for; and you shall put   66
This night's great business into my dispatch;   67
Which shall to all our nights and days to come
Give solely sovereign sway and masterdom.
Macbeth. We will speak further.
Lady Macbeth.   Only look up clear;   70
To alter favour ever is to fear.
Leave all the rest to me.   [*Exeunt.*

Scene six.

(THE SAME. BEFORE THE CASTLE)

Hautboys and torches. Enter DUNCAN, MALCOLM, DONALBAIN, BANQUO, LENNOX, MACDUFF, ROSS, ANGUS *and* Attendants.

Duncan. This castle hath a pleasant seat; the air   1
Nimbly and sweetly recommends itself
Unto our gentle senses.
Banquo.   This guest of summer,
The temple-haunting martlet, does approve   4
By his lov'd mansionry that the heaven's breath   5
Smells wooingly here: no jutty, frieze,   6
Buttress, nor coign of vantage, but this bird   7
Hath made his pendent bed and procreant cradle: 8
Where they most breed and haunt, I have observ'd
The air is delicate.

Enter LADY MACBETH

Duncan.   See, see, our honour'd hostess!
The love that follows us sometime is our trouble,   11
Which still we thank as love. Herein I teach you
How you shall bid God 'eyld us for your pains,
And thank us for your trouble.
Lady Macbeth.   All our service,
In every point twice done, and then done double,
Were poor and single business, to contend   16
Against those honours deep and broad wherewith
Your majesty loads our house: for those of old,
And the late dignities heap'd up to them,   19
We rest your hermits.
Duncan.   Where's the Thane of Cawdor?   20
We cours'd him at the heels, and had a purpose   21
To be his purveyor; but he rides well,   22
And his great love, sharp as his spur, hath holp him   23

---

57. "instant": the present moment.

62. "To beguile the time": to deceive the people of the time, or the world.

66. "provided for": attended to or, in other words, "murdered."

67. "This night's great business": the great thing that she is going to do—murder Duncan.
"dispatch": management.

70-1. "Only look . . . fear": your face (favor) changes and your feelings and actions are shown by your expression, we may be discovered.

1. "seat": setting, site, situation.

4. "The temple-haunting martlet": the martin makes its home in the steeples of churches.
"approve": prove, show.

5. "mansionry": house-building.
"heaven's breath": inviting air.

6. "jutty": projecting part.
"frieze": projection at the top of the columns in the building.

7. "coign of vantage": suitable corner for nesting.

8. "pendent bed": hanging nest.
"procreant cradle": the nest where the young are bred.

11-14. "The love . . . your trouble": a visit from the one we love gives us trouble, but we are thankful for the trouble because we know that they love us.

16. "single": weak.

16-17. "to contend Against": offset, vie with.

19. "late dignities": thaneship of Cawdor.

20. "We rest your hermits": we are your debtors and are bound to pray for you.

21. "cours'd": followed closely behind him, rode quickly behind him.

22. "purveyor": officer who prepares king's receptions on trips.

23. "holp": helped.

MACBETH

ACT I SCENE VII

This, Macbeth's first true soliloquy, is the second of a series of crucial speeches (the long aside in Scene Three was the first) in which Macbeth chooses in the light of events what role he will play, and devises a course of action to fit it. They should be minutely studied and, if possible, committed to memory, since so much of Macbeth's tragic stature hinges on them.

The difficulty of this soliloquy, its almost incoherence, reflects his unsorted impressions, which, in turn, are responsible for the negative nature of his conclusion. He has not enough time.

His opening line should be compared with Lady Macbeth's, "What's done is done" (III,ii,12) in the light of our comment on her character beside Scene Five.

He begins with a wish that the deed could have no result but success. Then he considers the afterlife. (Murder is a mortal sin). His willingness to face the prospect of damnation shows that his faith is weak; his imagination does not lend reality to the torments of hell. (King James said, "There is no kind of persons so subject to harm of them [i.e. witches] as these that are of infirm and weak faith.")

Next he turns to earthly consequences, which are more present to him, and which he fears.

The poisoned chalice is an important poetic symbol. The chalice is a wine goblet, especially that used in the communion service of the church. Now a poisoned chalice suggests the reversal of this mystery (the communion wine is the wine of life). Witches held from time to time, what they called the black mass, which was in fact the communion service blasphemously inverted. Thus the poisoned chalice is a companion-symbol to Lady Macbeth's prayer, "Come you spirits . . ." (I,v,39).

The rest is a catalogue of reasons of virtue against the deed. In picturing the horror and pity the country would feel, he sees a magnification of his own horror. Repugnance as well as fear deters him. His reflections might have continued further if Lady Macbeth's entrance had not interrupted him. Events do not cease to crowd his judgment.

His wife is, of course, the spur he lacked. The word is a poetic echo of I,vi, 23 ("And his great love, sharp as his spur . . .").

We must never forget line 31. This was Macbeth's own conclu-

To his home before us. Fair and noble hostess,
We are your guest to-night.
  Lady Macbeth.   Your servants ever
Have theirs, themselves, and what is theirs, in compt, 26
To make their audit at your highness' pleasure, 27
Still to return your own.
  Duncan.   Give me your hand; 28
Conduct me to mine host: we love him highly,
And shall continue our graces towards him. 30
By your leave, hostess.   [*Exeunt.* 31

Scene seven.

(THE SAME. A ROOM IN THE CASTLE)

Hautboys and torches. Enter, and pass over the stage, a Sewer, and divers Servants with dishes and service. Then, enter MACBETH.

Macbeth. If it were done when 'tis done, then 'twere 1
  well
It were done quickly; if the assassination 3
Could trammel up the consequence, and catch
With his surcease success; that but this blow 4
Might be the be-all and the end-all. Here, 5
But here, upon this bank and shoal of time, 6
We'd jump the life to come. But in these cases 7
We still have judgment here; that we but teach 8
Bloody instructions, which, being taught, return
To plague the inventor; this even-handed justice 10
Commends the ingredients of our poison'd chalice 11
To our own lips. He's here in double trust:
First, as I am his kinsman and his subject,
Strong both against the deed; then, as his host,
Who should against his murderer shut the door,
Not bear the knife myself. Besides, this Duncan
Hath borne his faculties so meek, hath been 17
So clear in his great office, that his virtues 18
Will plead like angels trumpet-tongu'd against
The deep damnation of his taking-off;
And pity, like a naked new-born babe, 21
Striding the blast, or heaven's cherubin, hors'd 22
Upon the sightless couriers of the air, 23
Shall blow the horrid deed in every eye,
That tears shall drown the wind. I have no spur 25
To prick the sides of my intent, but only
Vaulting ambition, which o'er-leaps itself 27
And falls on the other.—

    Enter LADY MACBETH.
        How now! what news?
Lady Macbeth. He has almost supp'd: why have
  you left the chamber?
Macbeth. Hath he ask'd for me? 29
Lady Macbeth.   Know you not he has?
Macbeth. We will proceed no further in this
  business:
He hath honour'd me of late; and I have bought 32

26. "in compt": on deposit, on account (something they do not own, but is entrusted to them).

27. "make their audit": render an account.

28. "Still": always.

30. "graces": royal favors.

31. "By your leave": permit me (he offers his arm to Lady Macbeth).

1-7. "If it were done . . . life to come": If the murder could be committed without any after effects or results then I would be glad to have it over with. If I could be sure of success and of the end of everything then it would be well if it were done.

3. "trammel up": catch as in a net.

4. "his surcease": Duncan's death.

5. "the be-all": everything, the whole thing.

6. "this bank and shoal of time": a man's lifetime is a mere sandbank or bar, soon to be covered by the sea of eternity.

7. "jump": disregard, jump over, risk eternity.

7-12. "But in these . . . own lips": We always have punishment in this life. If I were to murder Duncan someone would plan to murder me. If I gave Duncan poison, someone would try to poison me.

8. "still": always.
    "here": in this world.

10. "even-handed": giving each one exactly what he deserves.

11. "Commends": offers.
    "chalice": cup.

17. "borne his faculties so meek": performed his duties so humbly.

18. "clear": free from blame.

21. "And pity . . . babe": pity is like a babe because it touches our tenderness.

22. "Striding the blast": riding upon the storm, or the wind.

23. "sightless": invisible.
    "couriers of the air": winds.

25. "drown the wind": tears shall be as plentiful as raindrops which causes the winds to die down.
    "no spur": comparing himself to a rider.

27. "Vaulting ambition": he is comparing himself to a rider who leaps too quickly when mounting and then lands on the other side.

29. "chamber": the dining room, hall.

32. "bought": won.

MACBETH

ACT I SCENE VII

sion, whatever his motives for it.

Note the metaphor of new clothes and compare I,iii,108, 145 ("borrowed robes," "strange garments").

The adage referred to in line 45 is: "Catus amat pisces sed non vult tingere plantas" (The cat loves fish, but does not wish to wet his feet).

Courage is the basis of a soldier's self-respect. Macbeth's refined conception of manhood cannot stand against Lady Macbeth's logic.

This telling passage reminiscent of I,v, 39-52 ("take my milk for gall") puzzles students. Historically, Macbeth was Lady Macbeth's second husband; her child was by the first.

Note how she even turns his honor against his virtue.

As the resolution of this last line rings out, we can feel the boundaries shift in Macbeth's mind. Before, his will was uncommitted, and the division between good and evil was forming within his mind. Now his face is the boundary and will smile on the unsuspecting world as his castle wall has done. We will see later what has become of his conscience and his repugnance.

The tragic choice is now made. Why are we sympathetic to Macbeth?

Golden opinions from all sorts of people,
Which would be worn now in their newest gloss,   34
Not cast aside so soon.
    Lady Macbeth.   Was the hope drunk,   35
Wherein you dress'd yourself? hath it slept since,
And wakes it now, to look so green and pale
At what it did so freely? From this time
Such I account thy love. Art thou afeard   39
To be the same in thine own act and valour
As thou art in desire? Wouldst thou have that
Which thou esteem'st the ornament of life,   42
And live a coward in thine own esteem,   43
Letting 'I dare not' wait upon 'I would,'   44
Like the poor cat i' the adage?
    Macbeth.   Prithee, peace
I dare do all that may become a man;
Who dares do more is none.
    Lady Macbeth.   What beast was't, then,
That made you break this enterprise to me?   48
When you durst do it, then you were a man;
And, to be more than what you were, you would   50
Be so much more the man. Nor time nor place
Did then adhere, and yet you would make both: 52
They have made themselves, and that their fitness   53
          now
Does unmake you. I have given suck, and know   54
How tender 'tis to love the babe that milks me:
I would, while it was smiling in my face,
Have pluck'd my nipple from his boneless gums,
And dash'd the brains out, had I so sworn as you
Have done to this.
    Macbeth.   If we should fail,—
    Lady Macbeth.   We fail?   59
But screw your courage to the sticking-place,   60
And we'll not fail. When Duncan is asleep,
Whereto the rather shall his day's hard journey   62
Soundly invite him, his two chamberlains   63
Will I with wine and wassail so convince,   64
That memory, the warder of the brain,
Shall be a fume, and the receipt of reason   66
A limbeck only; when in swinish sleep
Their drenched natures lie, as in a death,   68
What cannot you and I perform upon
The unguarded Duncan? what not put upon
His spongy officers, who shall bear the guilt   71
Of our great quell?
    Macbeth.   Bring forth men-children only;   72
For thy undaunted mettle should compose   73
Nothing but males. Will it not be receiv'd,   74
When we have mark'd with blood those sleepy two
Of his own chamber and us'd their very daggers,
That they have done 't?
    Lady Macbeth.   Who dares receive it other,   77
As we shall make our griefs and clamour roar
Upon his death?
    Macbeth.   I am settled, and bend up   79
Each corporal agent to this terrible feat.
Away, and mock the time with fairest show: 81
False face must hide what the false heart doth know.
          [*Exeunt.*

25

34. "would": should.

35-7. "Was the hope," etc.: was your hope like a reveler who wakes the next morning green-faced and nauseated by the mere thought of last night's debauch?

39. "Such": just as fickle as your resolution has proved.

42. "the ornament of life": the crown the highest possession.

43. "And live a coward": do without it now and everafter accuse yourself of cowardice.

43. "esteem": opinion.

44. "wait upon": always follow, wait upon constantly.

48. "break": disclose.

50-1. "And, to be . . . man": by being more daring than you were then you would be more of a man.

52. "adhere": agree with the plan.

53. "have made ourselves": Duncan is now in our power.

54. "unmake": unnerve.

59. Here Malcolm drops the defense of scruples and tries to oppose the act on another ground—risk of failure.

60. "But": only.

62. "the rather": all the more.

62-63. "Whereto . . . him": his long journey will make him sleep soundly.

63. "chamberlains": grooms or body guards who slept by his bed.

64. "convince": overpower, overcome.

66. "receipt": receptacle.

68. "drenched": drowned.

71. "spongy": drunk, saturated with liquor.

72. "quell": murder, killing.

73. "mettle": quality.

74. "receiv'd": believed accepted as true.

77. "receive it other": take it otherwise.

79. "settled": resolute, determined.

79-80. "bend-up . . . agent": strain all the powers of my body.

81. "show": looks and bearings, appearance.

81. "mock the time": beguile or deceive the world.

MACBETH

ACT II SCENE I

In this scene we again have Banquo and Macbeth side by side for comparison. Its important elements are: the dark night, the relationship of Banquo and Macbeth, and Macbeth's second soliloquy. (The third in our series of crucial speeches.)

"Their candles" are of course the stars. The Prince of the Air (Satan) has given the Macbeths their wish. (See I,iv,50: "Stars hide your fires . . ." and I,v,49: "Come thick night . . .")

Banquo's character is enriched here by the fact that he too is tempted. His cursed thoughts are like Macbeth's "horrible imaginings" (I,iii,138). He rejects them from his consciousness which is not divided as Macbeth's was, but in sleep when consciousness does not function, he, too, is attacked by temptation so strongly that he would not (i.e., does not want to) sleep.

Fleance, a young boy, is symbolic of Banquo's line, ennobled by the witches. His tender weakness is itself a temptation to Macbeth.

Their conversation is like the sparring at the beginning of a bout. They try each other out. When Banquo reaffirms his loyalty and detachment from evil, a great gulf opens between Macbeth and him.

His drink is a convenient explanation for the servant's ear of the reason for the signal bell, but, like Lady Macbeth's raven, it is symbolic. His drink will be of blood; here is the contents of his "poisoned chalice" (I,vii,11). Communion wine represents the blood of Christ, and the community it unites is of everlasting life; the community of consumers of human blood (i.e., murderers) is of death both here and hereafter.

THE SOLILOQUY: In this famous speech he suppresses his imagination and siezes his resolve. He casts himself into the role of withered murder, in league with the forces of night. The dagger is his hallucination, produced by his imagination, intensified by his emotional exhaustion and strain so that its vision seems for a while real. The immediate effect of the vision is to cause a powerful re-

---

ACT TWO, scene one.

(INVERNESS. COURT WITHIN THE CASTLE)

Enter BANQUO *and* FLEANCE, *with a Servant bearing a torch before him.*

Banquo. How goes the night, boy?
Fleance. The moon is down; I have not heard the clock.
Banquo. And she goes down at twelve.
Fleance.   I take 't, 'tis later, sir. 3
Banquo. Hold, take my sword. There's husbandry in 4
heaven;
Their candles are all out. Take thee that too. 5
A heavy summons lies like lead upon me, 6
And yet I would not sleep: merciful powers!
Restrain in me the cursed thoughts that nature 8
Gives way to in repose.

Enter MACBETH, *and a Servant with a torch.*
     Give me my sword.—
Who's there?
Macbeth. A friend.
Banquo. What, sir! not yet at rest? The king's a-bed:
He hath been in unusual pleasure, and
Sent forth great largess to your offices. 14
This diamond he greets your wife withal, 15
By the name of most kind hostess; and shut up 16
In measureless content.
Macbeth.   Being unprepar'd,
Our will became the servant to defect, 18
Which else should free have wrought.
Banquo.   All's well.
I dreamt last night of the three weird sisters:
To you they have show'd some truth.
Macbeth.   I think not of them:
Yet, when we can entreat an hour to serve, 22
We would spend it in some words upon that business,
If you would grant the time.
Banquo.   At your kind'st leisure. 24
Macbeth. If you shall cleave to my consent, when 25
'tis,
It shall make honour for you.
Banquo.   So I lose none 26
In seeking to augment it, but still keep 27
My bosom franchis'd and allegiance clear, 28
I shall be counsell'd.
Macbeth.   Good repose the while! 29
Banquo. Thanks, sir: the like to you.
     [*Exeunt* BANQUO *and* FLEANCE.
Macbeth. Go bid thy mistress, when my drink is 31
ready
She strike upon the bell. Get thee to bed. 32
     [*Exit* Servant.
Is this a dagger which I see before me,

26

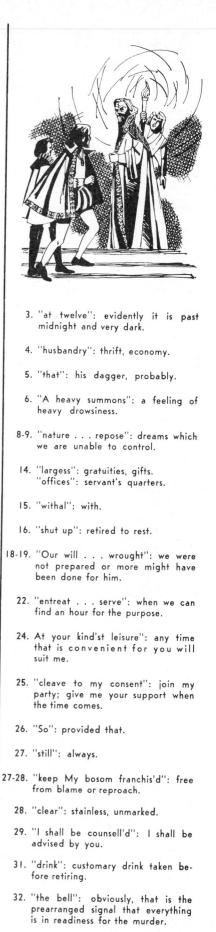

3. "at twelve": evidently it is past midnight and very dark.

4. "husbandry": thrift, economy.

5. "that": his dagger, probably.

6. "A heavy summons": a feeling of heavy drowsiness.

8-9. "nature . . . repose": dreams which we are unable to control.

14. "largess": gratuities, gifts. "offices": servant's quarters.

15. "withal": with.

16. "shut up": retired to rest.

18-19. "Our will . . . wrought": we were not prepared or more might have been done for him.

22. "entreat . . . serve": when we can find an hour for the purpose.

24. At your kind'st leisure": any time that is convenient for you will suit me.

25. "cleave to my consent": join my party; give me your support when the time comes.

26. "So": provided that.

27. "still": always.

27-28. "keep My bosom franchis'd": free from blame or reproach.

28. "clear": stainless, unmarked.

29. "I shall be counsell'd": I shall be advised by you.

31. "drink": customary drink taken before retiring.

32. "the bell": obviously, that is the prearranged signal that everything is in readiness for the murder.

MACBETH

ACT II SCENE I

coil, expressed in the past tenses of lines 42-3. His repugnance against evil and disorder, then, is still active, still able to divide his "single state of man"; but it has changed places. Where before it was the ally of his conscious effort to avoid temptation, now it is the enemy of his peace of mind having fallen. Note how his description of night turns to images of ugliness, reversal of nature, malice. Night is terrifying; in it evil things come to stealthy life. Natural men avoid the spectacle because they sleep then, unless, like Banquo, their sleep is troubled with dreams. Sleep and waking, and dreaming, (the middle state between them) become important symbolic elements in the play from now on.

Hecate was a Roman goddess of night, the moon, fortune, magic arts and spells, and the air. The heathen gods either vanished at Christ's birth (according to early Church doctrine) or became lieutenants of Satan. Thus Hecate was transposed into the guardian of witches. She was not part of popular folklore so much as sophisticated literature. Her mention by Shakespeare here may have given Middleton his cue for her appearance in the play. (See III,v and comment there.)

Tarquin, an Etruscan tyrant in Rome, raped Lucrece, the last virtuous matron in the city, after which she committed suicide. The tale was very popular in England and Shakespeare had written a narrative poem on the subject earlier in his career.

ACT II SCENE II

With the murder of Duncan the second stage of the plot reaches conclusion, and here just as in Scene Three of Act One the steady continuity of the march of events is maintained when the immediate results of the action lead forward the next stage.

The nervous tension of the scene is remarkable, stretched between fear of discovery and failure, the horror of the deed, and the flickering evidence of supernatural presences. It is a study in masterly pace and timing.

There is Holinshed's account (in the story of King Duffe) of the two chamberlains, "who came forth again (having seen the king safely to bed) and then fell to banqueting with Donwald and his wife, who had prepared divers delicate dishes and sundry sorts of drinks for their rear supper or collation,

---

The handle toward my hand? Come, let me clutch thee:
I have thee not, and yet I see thee still.
Art thou not, fatal vision, sensible   36
To feeling as to sight? or art thou but
A dagger of the mind, a false creation,
Proceeding from the heat-oppressed brain?   39
I see thee yet, in form as palpable   40
As this which now I draw.
Thou marshall'st me the way that I was going;   42
And such an instrument I was to use.
Mine eyes are made the fools o' the other senses,   44
Or else worth all the rest: I see thee still;
And on thy blade and dudgeon gouts of blood   46
Which was not so before. There's no such thing:
It is the bloody business which informs   48
Thus to mine eyes. Now o'er the one half-world
Nature seems dead, and wicked dreams abuse
The curtain'd sleep; witchcraft celebrates   51
Pale Hecate's offerings; and wither'd murder,   52
Alarum'd by his sentinel, the wolf,   53
Whose howl's his watch, thus with his stealthy pace,   54
With Tarquin's ravishing strides, toward his design
Moves like a ghost. Thou sure and firm-set earth,
Hear not my steps, which way they walk, for fear   57
Thy very stones prate of my whereabout,   58
And take the present horror from the time,
Which now suits with it. Whiles I threat, he lives: 60
Words to the heat of deeds too cold breath gives.   61
                                              [*A bell rings*

I go, and it is done; the bell invites me.
Hear it not, Duncan; for it is a knell
That summons thee to heaven or to hell.

Scene two.

(THE SAME)

Enter LADY MACBETH

Lady Macbeth. That which hath made them drunk   1
    hath made me bold,
What hath quench'd them hath given me fire. Hark!   2
    Peace!
It was the owl that shriek'd, the fatal bellman,   3
Which gives the stern'st good-night. He is about it: 4
The doors are open, and the surfeited grooms   5
Do mock their charge with snores: I have drugg'd   6
    their possets,
That death and nature do contend about them,   7
Whether they live or die.
Macbeth [*Within.*] Who's there? what, ho!
Lady Macbeth. Alack! I am afraid they have awak'd.
And 'tis not done; the attempt and not the deed   11
Confounds us. Hark! I laid their daggers ready;   12
He could not miss them. Had he not resembled
My father as he slept, I had done 't. My husband!

---

36. "fatal": fateful, ominous.
    "sensible": perceptible.

39. "heat-oppressed": capable of being handled.

42. "marshall'st me": urges me on.

44-45. "Mine eyes . . . rest": He is aware of the existence of the dagger only by the means of his eyes. Therefore, if it is mere fancy, then his eyes have become fools to be mocked at by his other senses; but if the dagger is real then his eyes are more trustworthy than all his other senses together.

46. "dudgeon": handle.
    "gouts": drops.

48. "informs": gives (false) information. "My murderous purpose presents this vision to my eyes."

51. "The curtain'd sleep": referring to a curtained bed or one curtained off from the room.

52. "Pale": Hecate was associated with the moon (Goddess of the moon). "Hecate": Queen of the witches, the classical goddess of the underworld and witchcraft.

52. "wither'd murder": murder pictured as an old man or possibly a ghost.

53. "Alarum'd": summoned to action.

54. "Whose howl's his watch": the wolf's howl for him like the cry of the night-watchman calling the hour.

57. "Hear not my steps . . . walk": do not hear the direction in which my steps are going.

58. "prate": chatter, gossip.

60. "threat": talk about murder.

61. "Words to the heat . . . gives": talking destroys the passion necessary to act.

1. "That": the wine.

2. "quench'd": stupefied.

3. "fatal bellman": see commentary opposite.
    "the owl": considered a bird of ill-omen.

4. "stern'st good-night": the warning good-night.

5. "surfeited": over-stuffed with food and drink.

6. "Do mock . . . snores": obviously they were asleep, a ridiculous way to keep watch.
    "possets": a drink made from hot curdled milk, ale, wine, etc., and taken usually on retiring.

7. "nature": life vital forces.

11-12. "the attempt . . . Confounds us": if he has failed in the attempt, we are ruined.

MACBETH

ACT II SCENE II

whereat they sat up so long, till they had charged their stomachs with such full gorges, that their heads were no sooner got to the pillow, but asleep they were so fast, that a man might have removed the chamber over them sooner than have awakened them out of their drunken sleep."

The owl was connected with witchcraft, as a form in which the devil often appeared to them. Its stealth, nocturnal habits, and blood-curdling shriek well fitted in for the role of bird of ill omen.

Reference to the fatal bellman provides us with an interesting topical allusion that aids our dating of the play. In 1605 Robert Dow set up a fund at St. Sepulchre's Church for bells to be rung in the night before prisoners in nearby Newgate Prison were to be executed. Besides tolling from the tower (within earshot of Shakespeare's lodgings), a sexton with a handbell was sent to ring it at the prison gates and recite verses bidding the condemned good night and exhorting them to repent and depend on the mercy of God. This charity caused much talk and ballads were written about it; its practice continued for 285 years, until 1890.

Here again (see I,vii,54-5) is evidence of the side of Lady Macbeth's nature that she tries to deny. It is a "compunctious visiting of nature" (I,v,44).

Crickets were supposed to cry out when a murder was done.

A hangman's task was a gory one. After the condemned man had been hanged, the body was quartered, and the entrails torn out and exhibited to the crowd.

Macbeth's inability to pray marks the finality of his separation from God's grace.

His sleeplessness stamps him unnatural, the fellow of Hecate and Tarquin, the wolf and the owl (see II,i,49-60).

He has asked for darkness; now he must live in it.

The washing of their hands, a practical necessity as Lady Macbeth insists, is a symbolical impossibility as Macbeth sees (II,ii,60-3; compare with Pontius Pilate; also see V,i).

The end of the event for Macbeth is remorse and self-loathing; he seems more afraid of himself than of discovery.

Against Macbeth's shaken "state of man," his wife imposes her hard-boiled intelligence with its rejection of the imagination (II.53-55) as illusion.

Enter MACBETH.

Macbeth. I have done the deed. Didst thou not hear a noise?

Lady Macbeth. I heard the owl scream and the   16
crickets cry.
Did not you speak?

Macbeth.   When?

Lady Macbeth.   Now.

Macbeth.   As I descended?

Lady Macbeth. Ay.

Macbeth. Hark!
Who lies i' the second chamber?

Lady Macbeth.   Donalbain.

Macbeth. [*Looking on his hands.*] This is a sorry   21
sight.

Lady Macbeth. A foolish thought to say a sorry sight.

Macbeth. There's one did laugh in 's sleep, and one   23
cried 'Murder!'
That they did wake each other: I stood and heard them;
But they did say their prayers, and address'd them   25
Again to sleep.

Lady Macbeth. There are two lodg'd together.

Macbeth. One cried 'God bless us!' and 'Amen'   27
the other:
As they had seen me with these hangman's hands.
Listening their fear, I could not say 'Amen,'   29
When they did say 'God bless us!'

Lady Macbeth.   Consider it not so deeply.

Macbeth. But wherefore could not I pronounce
'Amen'?
I had most need of blessing, and 'Amen'
Stuck in my throat.

Lady Macbeth.   These deeds must not be thought   33
After these ways; so, it will make us mad.

Macbeth. Methought I heard a voice cry 'Sleep no
more!
Macbeth does murder sleep,' the innocent sleep,
Sleep that knits up the ravell'd sleave of care,   37
The death of each day's life, sore labour's bath,   38
Balm of hurt minds, great nature's second course,
Chief nourisher in life's feast,—

Lady Macbeth.   What do you mean?   40

Macbeth. Still it cried, 'Sleep no more!' to all the
house:
'Glamis hath murder'd sleep, and therefore Cawdor   42
Shall sleep no more, Macbeth shall sleep no more!'

Lady Macbeth. Who was it that thus cried? Why,
worthy thane,
You do unbend your noble strength to think   45
So brainsickly of things. Go get some water,   46
And wash this filthy witness from your hand.   47
Why did you bring these daggers from the place?
They must lie there: go carry them, and smear
The sleepy grooms with blood.

Macbeth.   I'll go no more:
I am afraid to think what I have done;
Look on 't again I dare not.

Lady Macbeth.   Infirm of purpose!
Give me the daggers. The sleeping and the dead

16. "crickets cry": thought of as an omen of death.

21. "sorry": miserable.

23. "There's one," etc.: Macbeth goes on to tell of what he heard as he was passing a bedroom on the way back from Duncan's room.

25. "address'd them": applied themselves.

27. "God bless us!" and "Amen": marked the conclusion of the prayers just mentioned.

29. "Listening their fear": listening to their expressions of alarm.

30. "it": not the murder but his inability to say "amen." To say "amen" when one heard someone utter a blessing was habitual in those days.

33. "thought": regarded.

37. "knits up": straightens out.

"sleave": skein (of silk).

38. "sore labour's bath": as refreshing as a bath to a laborer after toiling.

40. "life's feast": life in two parts, food and sleep; sleep is more important.

42. The various titles show that this cry is in part an echo of the weird sisters' greeting.

45. "unbend": relax.

46. "brainsickly": foolishly.

47. "witness": evidence.

MACBETH

ACT II SCENE III

In most of Shakespeare's plays, subplots and comic episodes interrupt to relieve or diversify the main action. In MACBETH this speech of the porter is the single example in a play that is otherwise austerely to the point. Granted that some time had to elapse before the gate was opened, why spend it with a drunken clown? The scene of discovery following makes a new kind of demand on Macbeth, and has a different kind of excitement. The listening strain of the murder scene must be cancelled and released before new action begins. The laughter which greets the porter's remarks in the theater is not simply amusement; there is a shrillness to it. The audience welcomes the opportunity to shout to relieve its feelings. Thus the playwright prevents emotional cramp from setting in.

The speech is symbolically true to the play's theme, and so keeps unity. Drunk, unkempt, and asleep late, the porter is a walking picture of disorder. In posing as the porter of hell-gate, he unconsciously speaks more truth than he knows.

THE FARMER: It was a common and generally detested practice to hoard grain in time of plenty when prices were low, in hopes of making a killing at exorbitant price in a year when the harvest failed. Some men whose fortunes depended on a famine had actually committed suicide when the harvest unexpectedly was bountiful.
THE EQUIVOCATOR: (We should call it double talk.) The Jesuit doctrine of equivocation held that the sin of lying lay not in misleading your hearers but in speaking what COULD not be true. Thus they held it no sin to utter any deceiving remark as long as it could from some viewpoint be true (e.g. WITNESS: [aloud] I was in the bank at the time and saw the robbery; I did not see the defendant there. [to himself] I saw only his clothing because he had a mask on).

Are but as pictures; 'tis the eye of childhood 54
That fears a painted devil. If he do bleed,
I'll gild the faces of the grooms withal; 56
For it must seem their guilt.
                  [Exit. Knocking within.
Macbeth.   Whence is that knocking? 57
How is 't with me, when every noise appals me?
What hands are here! Ha! they pluck out mine eyes.
Will all great Neptune's ocean wash this blood
Clean from my hand? No, this my hand will rather
The multitudinous seas incarnadine, 62
Making the green one red. 63

Re-enter LADY MACBETH.

Lady Macbeth. My hands are of your colour, but I
   shame
To wear a heart so white.—[*Knocking within.*] I hear
   a knocking
At the south entry; retire we to our chamber; 66
A little water clears us of this deed;
How easy is it, then! Your constancy 68
Hath left you unattended. [*Knocking within.*] Hark! 69
   more knocking.
Get on your night-gown, lest occasion call us, 70
And show us to be watchers. Be not lost
So poorly in your thoughts. 72
Macbeth. To know my deed 'twere best not know 73
   myself.
                  [Knocking within.
Wake Duncan with thy knocking! I would thou
   couldst!
                  [Exeunt.

Scene three.

(THE SAME)

Knocking within. Enter a Porter.

Porter. Here's a knocking indeed! If a man were porter of hell-gate, he should have old turning the key. 2
[*Knocking within.*] Knock, knock, knock! Who's there, i' the name of Beelzebub? Here's a farmer that 4
hanged himself on the expectation of plenty; come in 5
time; have napkins enough about you; here you'll 6
sweat for 't. [*Knocking within.*] Knock, knock! Who's there, i' the other devil's name! Faith, here's an equivo- 8
cator, that could swear in both the scales against either scale; who committed treason enough for God's sake, yet could not equivocate to heaven: O! come in, equivo- 11
cator. [*Knocking within.*] Knock, knock, knock! Who's there? Faith, here's an English tailor come hither for 13
stealing out of a French hose: come in, tailor; here you may roast your goose. [*Knocking within.*] Knock, 15
knock; never at quiet! What are you? But this place is too cold for hell. I'll devil-porter it no further: I had 17
thought to have let in some of all professions, that go the primrose way to the everlasting bonfire. [*Knocking within.*] Anon, anon! I pray you, remember the porter. 20
                  [Opens the gate.

---

54. "as pictures": just as harmless as pictures.

56. "gild": stain or smear.

57. "within" (stage directions): behind the scenes.

62. "multitudinous": referring to many big waves.

62. "incarnadine": turn blood-red.
63. "Making the green one red": turning the green color of the sea into one universal red.

66. "entry": entrance.

68-69. "Your . . . unattended": your usual firmness is gone.

70. "night-gown": dressing gown.

"lest occasion call us": lest we are called on.

72. "So poorly": in such a poor-spirited way.

73. "To know my deed": if I must know my deed; must feel my crime to the full.

2. "should": certainly would.

2. "have old": have a great deal of trouble (a slang term).

4. "Beelzebub": a name for Satan.

5-6. "come in time": your arrival is opportune.

6. "napkins": handkerchiefs.

8-9. "equivocator": one who purposely makes misleading statements.

11. "equivocate to heaven": get himself into heaven by equivocation.

13-14. "tailor . . . hose": French hose (i.e., breeches) were tight fitting and would make it difficult to embezzle any cloth from them.

15. "goose": tailor's iron.

17. "devil-porter it": act the part of a demon porter at hell-gate.

20. "Anon, anon": In a moment!

20. "remember the porter": he expects a tip.

MACBETH

ACT II SCENE III

Macbeth's remarks in this scene down to line 54 are good examples. It was a welcome doctrine to English Catholics whose religion was outlawed and who could not live in England without "swearing and lying," i.e., perjury (see IV,ii, 47). The doctrine was important news in England from February to May, 1606, owing to the examination, trial, and execution of Henry Garnet, Superior of the English Jesuits. His treason lay in preaching illegally, and in aiding the Gunpowder Plot by falsely denying his knowledge of it. He said in his examination that he was guilty if equivocation could not save him, and a lengthy discussion of the doctrine was part of his trial. The phrase, "treason enough for God's sake" is descriptive of Garnet, who was devout and sincere. FRENCH HOSE: It came in two styles, round (i.e., very full), and tight. A few yards of cloth snipped out of a round hose (hose by the way are like breeches) might not be missed. Line 54 echoes with poignant contrast, "Tomorrow, as he purposes" (I,v,59.)

Compare Lennox's account of the night's disturbances with that of Ross and the old man in II,iv. Belief in such natural disturbances accompanying important human events (just as a stone dropped in a pool sends ripples all over its surface) was based on the very old idea of the unity of all creation which lent credibility to astrology, and through which God must be conscious of the sparrow's fall (cf. the earthquake accompanying the crucifixion). That the belief was not dead, the following news item of February, 1606, bears witness: "The sun (in Carlstadt) shone like blood nine days; two armies seen in the air in battle; a woman delivered of three sons, one with four heads that spake and uttered strange things, one black, one like death. Such things together with the Earth's and Moon's late and horrible obscuration, the frequent eclipsation of the fixed bodies (stars), within these four years more than ordinary betoken new leagues, traitorous designments, catching at kingdoms, translation of empire, downfall of men in authority, emulation, ambition, innovations, factions, sects, schisms, and much disturbance."

Holinshed (concerning Duffe's death) has: "Such outrageous winds arose with lightnings and tempests that people were in great fear of present destruction."

The obscure bird is, again, the owl.

Enter MACDUFF *and* LENNOX.

Macduff. Was it so late, friend, ere you went to bed 21
That you lie so late?
Porter. Faith, sir, we were carousing till the second
cock. And drink, sir, is a great provoker of three 23
things.
Macduff. What three things does drink especially provoke?
Porter. Marry, sir, nose-painting, sleep, and urine.
Lechery, sir, it provokes and unprovokes. It provokes
the desire, but it takes away the performance. Therefore much drink may be said to be an equivocator with
lechery. It makes him and it mars him, it sets him on
and it takes him off, it persuades him and disheartens
him, makes him stand to and not stand to; in conclusion, equivocates him in a sleep and giving him the lie,
leaves him.
Macduff. I believe drink gave thee the lie last night.
Porter. That it did sir, i' the very throat on me. But I
requited him for his lie; and, I think, being too strong
for him, though he took up my legs sometime, yet I
made a shift to cast him.
Macduff. Is thy master stirring?

Enter MACBETH

Our knocking has awak'd him; here he comes.
Lennox. Good morrow, noble sir.
Macbeth. Good morrow, both.
Macduff. Is the king stirring, worthy thane?
Macbeth. Not yet.
Macduff. He did command me to call timely on him: 44
I have almost slipp'd the hour.
Macbeth. I'll bring you to him. 46
Macduff. I know this is a joyful trouble to you;
But yet 'tis one.
Macbeth. The labour we delight in physics pain. 49
This is the door.
Macduff. I'll make so bold to call,
For 'tis my limited service. (Exit. 52
Lennox. Goes the king hence today?
Macbeth. He does: he did appoint so. 54
Lennox. The night has been unruly: where we lay,
Our chimneys were blown down; and, as they say,
Lamentings heard i' the air; strange screams of death, 57
And prophesying with accents terrible
Of dire combustion and confus'd events 59
New hatch'd to the woeful time. The obscure bird 60
Clamour'd the livelong night; some say the earth
Was feverous and did shake.
Macbeth. 'Twas a rough night.
Lennox. My young remembrance cannot parallel
A fellow to it.

Re-enter MACDUFF.

Macduff. O horror! horror! horror! Tongue nor heart
Cannot conceive nor name thee!
Macbeth.
        What's the matter?
Lennox.
Macduff. Confusion now hath made his masterpiece! 67
Most sacrilegious murder hath broke ope
The Lord's anointed temple, and stole hence 69
The life o' the building!
Macbeth. What is 't you say? the life?

21. "so late": it is early in the morning, but it is late for the porter to be on duty.

23. "the second cock": about two in the morning.

44. "timely": early.

46. "slipp'd the hour": passed the appointed time.
"bring": escort, conduct.

49. "physics": cures.

52. "limited": appointed.

54. "appoint": arrange, plan.

57. "Lamentings . . . air": such prodigies were supposed to announce the death of great men.

59. "combustion": tumult and disorder in the state.

60. "New hatch'd to the woeful time": born especially for this terrible time.
"The obscure bird": the owl.

67. "Confusion": destruction.

69. "The Lord's anointed temple": the body of Duncan, who, as king, is the Lord's anointed.

MACBETH

Note the lovely irony of lines 86-9.

Malcolm's "O, by whom?" frequently appears comic to the reader. This is one of those lines that needs the art of the actor to fill it out. Malcolm is shocked, struck dumb. How would you speak it on the stage?

Macduff is immediately suspicious of Macbeth's removal of the only possible witness, and Macbeth's over-elaborate defense of himself, windy with rhetoric, looks like landing him further in hot water when Lady Macbeth's swoon saves the situation. The question is whether she really fainted or not. It will never be solved.

Lennox. Mean you his majesty?

Macduff. Approach the chamber, and destroy your sight

With a new Gorgon: do not bid me speak; 74

See, and then speak yourselves.

        (Exeunt MACBETH *and* LENNOX.

Awake! awake!

Ring the alarum-bell. Murder and treason!

Banquo and Donalbain! Malcolm! awake!

Shake off this downy sleep, death's counterfeit, 79

And look on death itself! up, up, and see

The great doom's image! Malcolm! Banquo! 81

As from your graves rise up, and walk like sprites, 82

To countenance this horror! Ring the bell.

        (Bell rings. 83

Enter LADY MACBETH.

Lady Macbeth. What's the business,

That such a hideous trumpet calls to parley 85

The sleepers of the house? speak, speak!

  Macduff. O gentle lady!

'Tis not for you to hear what I can speak;

The repetition in a woman's ear 88

Would murder as it fell.

Enter BANQUO.

O Banquo! Banquo!

Our royal master's murder'd!

  Lady Macbeth. Woe, alas!

What! in our house?

  Banquo. Too cruel any where.

Dear Duff, I prithee, contradict thyself,

And say it is not so.

Re-enter MACBETH and LENNOX

Macbeth. Had I but died an hour before this chance 94

I had liv'd a blessed time; for, from this instant,

There's nothing serious in mortality, 96

All is but toys; renown and grace is dead, 97

The wine of life is drawn, and the mere lees

Is left this vault to brag of. 99

Enter MALCOLM and DONALBAIN.

Donalbain. What is amiss?

Macbeth. You are, and do not know 't: 100

The spring, the head, the fountain of your blood

Is stopp'd; the very source of it is stopp'd.

  Macduff. Your royal father's murder'd.

  Malcolm. O! by whom?

  Lennox. Those of his chamber, as it seem'd, had done 't:

Their hands and faces were all badg'd with blood; 105

So were their daggers, which unwip'd we found

Upon their pillows: they star'd, and were distracted; 107

   no man's life

Was to be trusted with them.

  Macbeth. O! yet I do repent me of my fury. 109

That I did kill them.

  Macduff. Wherefore did you so?

  Macbeth. Who can be wise, amaz'd, temperate and furious,

Loyal and neutral, in a moment? No man:

The expedition of my violent love 113

Outran the pauser, reason. Here lay Duncan,

His silver skin lac'd with his golden blood; 115

And his gash'd stabs look'd like a breach in nature 116

31

74 "Gorgon": in Greek mythology the Gorgons were three sisters: to look at them turned one to stone.

79 "death's counterfeit": the image or picture of death.

81 "great doom's image": a sight as terrible as the day of judgment.

82 "As . . . graves": Macduff dwells upon the thought of the day of judgment.
   "sprites": spirits, ghosts.

83 "countenance": be in keeping with

85 "parley": conference.

88 "repetition": recital, report.

94 "chance": event.

96 "nothing . . . mortality": nothing worthwhile in human life.

97 "toys": trifles.
   "grace": goodness, virtue.

99 "vault": may mean both the heavens and a wine cellar.

100 "You are": you are amiss, i.e., you are missing a father—a play on "amiss."

105 "badg'd": marked as with a badge.

107 "they star'd . . . distracted": that is, when roused from their drugged sleep, Macbeth then killed them before they could say a word.

109 "yet": even so.

113-4 "The expedition . . . reason": the strength of my love made me act hastily instead of using reason. Reason would have made me pause.

115 "silver skin": a vivid picture of deathly pallor.
   "lac'd": streaked as with lace.

116 "breach in nature": the stabs looked like breeches in a fortress.

MACBETH

ACT II SCENE III

Banquo's sturdy affirmation of faith (complimentary again to King James's ancestor) is like a rock of order in a sea of confusion. The disorder both of dress and action is symbolic as well as dramatic, and should be visualized.

ACT II SCENE IV

This scene rounds off the act by dealing with the immediate results of Duncan's death.

The old man represents the people of Scotland, affected by the action, though they are not part of it. It is an important enlargement of the scope of the action if we are aware of these people whose fortunes are determined by those of their rulers. The old man's age and saintly character (Ross speaks to him with respect although he is a commoner) fit him to represent orderly and godly civilization, to speak from the point of view of balance and moderation.

For ruin's wasteful entrance: there, the murderers,
Steep'd in the colours of their trade, their daggers
Unmannerly breech'd with gore: who could refrain,   119
That had a heart to love, and in that heart
Courage to make's love known?
  Lady Macbeth. Help me hence, ho!
  Macduff. Look to the lady.   122
  Malcolm. (Aside to DONALBAIN.) Why do we hold
    our tongues,
That most may claim this argument for ours?   124
  Donalbain. (Aside to MALCOLM.) What should be
    spoken
Here where our fate, hid in an auger-hole,   126
May rush and seize us? Let's away: our tears   127
Are not yet brew'd.
  Malcolm. (Aside to DONALBAIN.) Nor our strong
    sorrow
Upon the foot of motion.
  Banquo. Look to the lady: 130
          (LADY MACBETH is carried out.
And when we have our naked frailties hid,   131
That suffer in exposure, let us meet,
And question this most bloody piece of work,   133
To know it further. Fears and scruples shake us: 134
In the great hand of God I stand, and thence
Against the undivulg'd pretence I fight   136
Of treasonous malice.
  Macduff. And so do I.
  All. So all.
  Macbeth. Let's briefly put on manly readiness, 138
And meet i' the hall together.
  All. Well contented.
    (*Exeunt all but* MALCOLM *and* DONALBAIN.
  Malcolm. What will you do? Let's not consort with
    them:
To show an unfelt sorrow is an office
Which the false man does easy. I'll to England.   142
  Donalbain. To Ireland, I; our separated fortune
Shall keep us both the safer: where we are,
There's daggers in men's smiles: the near in blood, 145
The nearer bloody.
  Malcolm. This murderous shaft that's shot
Hath not yet lighted, and our safest way
Is to avoid the aim: therefore, to horse;
And let us not be dainty of leave-taking,
But shift away: there's warrant in that theft   150
Which steals itself when there's no mercy left.
                      (*Exeunt*

Scene four.

(THE SAME. WITHOUT THE CASTLE.)

Enter ROSS *and an* OLD MAN.

Old Man. Threescore and ten I can remember well;   1
Within the volume of which time I have seen   2
Hours dreadful and things strange, but this sore   3
  night

119 "breech'd": covered as with breeches.

122 "Look to the lady": Malcolm and Donalbain take advantage of the confusion that follows to exchange a few words.

124 "That . . . ours": who have the best right to talk on the subject.

126 "hid in an auger-hole": coming from a source so small that we may not suspect its presence.

127 "tears . . . brew'd": we are not yet ready to shed tears. This is sarcastic. They suspect Macbeth's feigned grief.

130 "Upon . . . motion": ready to express itself.

131 "naked frailties": shivering. scantily clad bodies.

133 "question": investigate.

134 "scruples": doubts, vague suspicions.

136 "undivulg'd pretence" etc.: the as yet undiscovered purpose of malicious traitors.

138 "manly readiness": our clothes—contrasts with "naked frailties."

142 "the false man" i.e., any false man. They suspect everybody.

145 "the near . . . bloody": the closer one of these nobles is to us in kinship, the more likely is he to murder us.

150 "shift away": steal away unperceived.

150-1 A man has a right to steal when he takes away merely himself from a place of danger.

1. The benign and dignified figure of the old man serves as a kind of chorus to the tragedy.

2. "volume": time is compared to a book.

3. "sore": dreadful.

MACBETH

ACT II SCENE IV

The strange events discussed (cf. II,iii, 55-63 and commentary) provide a nice example of how Shakespeare adapts history to his purpose, in this case symbolic. Here is Holinshed: "Monstrous sights that were seen within the Scottish kingdom that year (of Duffe's death) were these: horses in Louthian, being of singular beauty and swiftness, did eat their own flesh . . . there was a sparhawk also strangled by an owl . . . For the space of six months together after this heinous murder there appeared no sun by day, nor moon by night in any part of the realm, but still the sky covered with continual cloud." The horses are made directly symbolic of discord between Duncan's thanes (disorder again), and the hawk is exchanged for the more kingly bird, Macbeth being thus identified with the owl.

Now that Macbeth is king, the boundary of evil has spread to darken his whole realm. Note the symbolic emphasis of "living light."

Macbeth has achieved his desire, but now must enjoy it in the company of his outraged imagination, his country's disturbance, the suspicious enmity of Macduff, and Banquo's virtue.

Hath trifled former knowings.
Ross.   Ah! good father, 4
Thou seest, the heavens, as troubled with man's act,
Threaten his bloody stage: by the clock 'tis day, 6
And yet dark night strangles the travelling lamp. 7
Is 't night's predominance, or the day's shame, 8
That darkness does the face of earth entomb,
When living light should kiss it?
Old Man.   'Tis unnatural,
Even like the deed that's done. On Tuesday last,
A falcon, towering in her pride of place, 12
Was by a mousing owl hawk'd at and kill'd.
Ross. And Duncan's horses,—a thing most strange
and certain,—
Beauteous and swift, the minions of their race, 15
Turn'd wild in nature, broke their stalls, flung out, 16
Contending 'gainst obedience, as they would
Make war with mankind.
Old Man.   'Tis said they eat each other. 18
Ross. They did so, to the amazement of mine eyes, 19
That look'd upon 't. Here comes the good Macduff.

Enter MACDUFF.

How goes the world, sir, now?
Macduff.   Why, see you not? 21
Ross. Is 't known who did this more than bloody
deed?
Macduff. Those that Macbeth hath slain.
Ross.   Alas, the day!
What good could they pretend?
Macduff.   They were suborn'd. 24
Malcolm and Donalbain, the king's two sons,
Are stol'n away and fled, which put upon them
Suspicion of the deed.
Ross.   'Gainst nature still! 27
Thriftless ambition, that wilt ravin up 28
Thine own life's means! Then 'tis most like
The sovereignty will fall upon Macbeth.
Macduff. He is already nam'd, and gone to Scone 31
To be invested.
Ross.   Where is Duncan's body? 32
Macduff. Carried to Colmekill, 33
The sacred storehouse of his predecessors 34
And guardian of their bones.
Ross.   Will you to Scone?
Macduff. No cousin, I'll to Fife. 36
Ross.   Well, I will thither.
Macduff. Well, may you see things well done
there: adieu!
Lest our old robes sit easier than our new! 38
Ross. Farewell, father.
Old Man. God's benison go with you: and with 40
those
That would make good of bad, and friends of foes!
                                        [*Exeunt.*

4. "trifled . . . knowings": made all my previous experience trivial.

6. "his bloody stage": earth, on which man performs murder.

7. "travelling lamp": the sun.

8-10. "Is 't . . . kiss it": Is the darkness due to Night's having become more powerful than Day or to Day's hiding his face in shame?

12. "towering . . . place": soaring proudly at the very highest position of flight.

15. "minions": darlings.

16. "flung out": kicked and plunged wildly.

18. "eat": past tense of "eat"; pronounced "et."

19. "amazement": stupefaction.

21. Macduff's vague feelings of uneasiness and suspicion are shown in his short, dry answers.

24. "pretend": intend to gain for themselves.

24. "suborn'd": secretly induced or hired.

27. "'Gainst nature still": continuing the old man's thoughts in line 10.

28-9. "Thriftless . . . means!": ambition that will plunder its own means of livelihood is unwise.

31. "nam'd": elected (by the council of nobles).

31. "Scone": where Scottish kings were crowned.

32. "invested": clother with sovereignty at the coronation.

33. "Colmekill": (St. Columba's Call) on the island of Iona, one of the Western Isles, and among the most ancient Christian communities in Britain. Traditional burial place for the Scottish kings.

34. "storehouse": burial place.

36. "Fife": Macduff's own home.

36. "thither": to Scone.

38. "Lest . . . new": we may not, I fear, be as happy under the new ruler as under the old.

40. "benison": blessing.

40-1. "and with . . . foes": and with all other unsuspecting persons who, like you, insist upon regarding bad men as good and friends as foes.

MACBETH

Act Three centers around the banquet through which Macbeth hopes to enlist the friendship of the thanes. The theme is introduced as soon as Macbeth enters. Again you must visualize the scene, especially the royal magnificence (cf. I,iv) of the "borrowed" robes.

Banquo seems here to be consciously toying with his temptation in a speech sending our memories back to the witches, and Macbeth's lines, "This supernatural soliciting/Cannot be ill . . . Why hath it given me earnest of success, /Commencing in a truth?" (I,iii, 130-42).

The discussion between Banquo and Macbeth seems like a continuation of that in II,i, only this time Banquo is perhaps the more cagey of the two. A splendid opportunity is offered the actor in Macbeth's so pointed questions.

Here is Macbeth's third soliloquy, the fourth in our series of speeches wherein he defines the role he will accept. With each successive one his range of choice is smaller, as the web of his destiny closes in. Now his restless desire has fixed itself upon security,

ACT THREE, scene one.

(FORRES. A ROOM IN THE PALACE)
Enter BANQUO.

Banquo. Thou hast it now: King, Cawdor, Glamis, all,
As the weird women promis'd; and, I fear,
Thou play'dst most foully for 't; yet it was said
It should not stand in thy posterity,   4
But that myself should be the root and father
Of many kings. If there come truth from them,—
As upon thee, Macbeth, their speeches shine,—   7
Why, by the verities on thee made good,   8
May they not be my oracles as well,   9
And set me up in hope? But, hush! no more.   10
    Sennet sounded. Enter MACBETH, *as king*; LADY
    MACBETH, *as queen*; LENNOX, ROSS, Lords,
    Ladies, *and* Attendants.
Macbeth. Here's our chief guest.
Lady Macbeth.   If he had been forgotten,
It had been as a gap in our great feast,
And all-thing unbecoming.   13
    Macbeth. To-night we hold a solemn supper, sir,   14
And I'll request your presence.
    Banquo.   Let your highness
Command upon me; to the which my duties   16
Are with a most indissoluble tie
For ever knit.
    Macbeth. Ride you this afternoon?   19
    Banquo. Ay, my good lord.
    Macbeth. We should have else desir'd your good
      advice —
Which still hath been both grave and prosperous—   22
In this day's council; but we'll take to-morrow.
Is 't far you ride?
    Banquo. As far, my lord, as will fill up the time
'Twixt this and supper; go not my horse the better,   26
I must become a borrower of the night
For a dark hour or twain.
    Macbeth.   Fail not our feast.
    Banquo. My lord, I will not.
    Macbeth. We hear our bloody cousins are bestow'd   30
In England and in Ireland, not confessing
Their cruel parricide, filling their hearers   32
With strange invention; but of that to-morrow,   33
When therewithal we shall have cause of state   34
Craving us jointly. Hie you to horse; adieu   35
Till you return at night. Goes Fleance with you?
    Banquo. Ay, my good lord; our time does call   37
    upon 's.
    Macbeth. I wish your horses swift and sure of foot;
And so I do commend you to their backs.   39
Farewell.   [*Exit* BANQUO.
Let every man be master of his time
Till seven at night; to make society   42
The sweeter welcome, we will keep ourself
Till supper-time alone; while then, God be with you!

---

4. "stand . . . posterity": remain with your descendants.

7. "their . . . shine": their prophecies were brilliantly fulfilled.

8. "verities": prophecies come true.

9. "oracles": supernatural speeches foretelling the future. They were commonly consulted in Graeco-Roman times, and were famous for the ambiguity of their messages.

10. Stage direction: "Sennet": a fanfare.

13. "all-thing": altogether, quite.

14. "solemn supper": a supper of ceremony, a state supper.

16. "Command": in emphatic contrast with Macbeth's word "request."

19. In the dialogue that follows, Macbeth camouflages his three questions "Ride you this afternoon," etc., with compliments.

22. "still": always.

22. "grave and prosperous": weighty and successful.

26-8. "go . . . twain": Unless my horse goes too fast to make it necessary, I shall have to continue my ride an hour or two after dark.

30. "cousins": Malcolm and Donalbain.
"bestow'd": taken refuge.

32. "parricide": father-murder.

33. "strange invention": fictitious stories of the murder.

34. "therewithal": besides that.
"cause of state": public business.

35. "Craving us jointly": requiring both your attention and mine.

37. "our time . . . upon's": time summons us to depart.

39. "commend you": entrust you with my best wishes.

42-4. "to make . . . alone": In order that your society may be all the more agreeable to me, I will deprive myself of it for a time.

MACBETH

ACT III SCENE I

which he seeks to gain by intriguing at the death of Banquo and Fleance (seemingly so easy to kill). Working himself up to this, he quells any compunction by intoxicating himself with malice. We see in lines 65-9 what has become of his conscience. His guilt is a high price that he has paid for success. It is unalterable ("What's done is done" III,ii,12). Having paid this price it would be folly to stop at one more crime which would secure his purchase.

The most striking thing of all is his design to frustrate the prophecy of the witches to Banquo. This amounts to defying the devil, a dangerous action for a man already committed to his communion. It must seem to Macbeth that his own action has secured the crown, since he did not wait for chance to crown him. And the power he now feels his exists to be employed in its own increase.

The throne he has gained is not enough; it is "fruitless," "barren." With the thought of the brevity of his sway comes desire to extend it into the future in the descendants he expects ("Bring forth men children only . . ." [I,vii,72]), and thus to triumph over time and fate.

In Banquo's royalty of nature, valor, and wisdom, we see King James's ancestry praised anew.

In the "vessel of his peace" we recall his "drink" (II,i,31) and the poisoned chalice I,vii,11).

Macbeth enters into deceitful persuasion of the two murders with considerable relish, marshalling rhetoric, insinuation, and veiled promise of favor until he sees he has won them; then cutting them short, finally ending with the greatest air of self-satisfaction.

[*Exeunt all but* MACBETH *and an Attendant.*

Sirrah, a word with you. Attend those men 45
Our pleasure?
  Attendant. They are, my lord, without the palace gate.
  Macbeth. Bring them before us. [*Exit* Attendant]
    To be thus is nothing; 48
But to be safely thus. Our fears in Banquo
Stick deep, and in his royalty of nature
Reigns that which would be fear'd: 'tis much he dares, 51
And, to that dauntless temper of his mind, 52
He hath a wisdom that doth guide his valour
To act in safety. There is none but he
Whose being I do fear; and under him
My genius is rebuk'd, as it is said 56
Mark Antony's was by Caesar. He chid the sisters 57
When first they put the name of king upon me,
And bade them speak to him; then, prophet-like,
They hail'd him father to a line of kings.
Upon my head they plac'd a fruitless crown,
And put a barren sceptre in my gripe,
Thence to be wrench'd with an unlineal hand, 63
No son of mine succeeding. If 't be so,
For Banquo's issue have I fil'd my mind; 65
For them the gracious Duncan have I murder'd;
Put rancours in the vessel of my peace 67
Only for them; and mine eternal jewel 68
Given to the common enemy of man, 69
To make them kings, the seed of Banquo kings!
Rather than so, come fate into the list, 71
And champion me to the utterance! Who's there? 72

Re-enter Attendant, *with two* Murderers.

Now go to the door, and stay there till we call.
             [*Exit* Attendant
Was it not yesterday we spoke together?
  First Murderer. It was, so please your highness.
  Macbeth.   Well then, now
Have you consider'd of my speeches? Know
That it was he in the times past which held you 77
So under fortune, which you thought had been 78
Our innocent self. This I made good to you 79
In our last conference, pass'd in probation with you, 80
How you were borne in hand, how cross'd, the instruments, 81
Who wrought with them, and all things else that might
To half a soul and to a notion craz'd 83
Say, 'Thus did Banquo.'
  First Murderer.   You made it known to us. 84
  Macbeth. I did so; and went further, which is now
Our point of second meeting. Do you find 86
Your patience so predominant in your nature
That you can let this go? Are you so gospell'd 88
To pray for this good man and for his issue, 89
Whose heavy hand hath bow'd you to the grave
And beggar'd yours for ever?
  First Murderer.   We are men, my liege. 91
  Macbeth. Ay, in the catalogue ye go for men; 92

35

45. "Sirrah": often used in addressing a servant, inferior, or child.

48. "To be thus": to be King.

51. "would be": requires to be.

52. "to that": in addition to.

56. "genius": it was believed that each person possessed a controlling genius (spirit) which directed his actions.
"rebuk'd": put to shame, abashed.

57. According to Plutarch's "Life of Antony," a soothsayer told Antony that his good angel and spirit was courageous when alone, but fearful when near Caesar's guiding spirit.

63. "with": by.

65. "fil'd": defiled.

67. "rancours": the deepest enmity or spite. The figure is of a vessel of wholesome liquid into which poison has been poured.

68. "mine eternal jewel": my soul.

69. "common enemy of man": enemy common to all men, i.e., the devil.

71. "list": the enclosed ground where tournaments were fought.

72. "champion me to the utterance": Fight on my side to the death. (A tricky passage to pin down.) This reading is the traditional meaning which the word "champion" had. But the witches represent fate, and they declared that Banquo's descendants should reign. In saying this line Macbeth seems to deny the necessity of their prophecy, or that they have power over the future. Chance did not crown him, after all; he did the murder himself, and the thanes elected him king because he was the natural successor in Malcolm's disgrace. Some scholars give Shakespeare credit for being the first to use the word champion with the opposite to its usual meaning, and accept the reading that Macbeth is defying fate.

77-8. "held . . . fortune": thwarted your careers.

79. "made good": proved.

80. "pass'd . . . you": I reviewed the facts with you and gave you proofs.

81. "borne in hand": to be dealt with hypocritically.
"instruments": documents.

83. "notion": mind.

84. "Banquo": with this word we learn for the first time whom Macbeth has been accusing.

86. "Our . . . meeting": the purpose of this second meeting.

88. "so gospell'd": so imbued with the spirit of the gospel, i.e., love your enemies, etc.

89. "for his issue": a significant addition.

91. "yours": your families and descendants.

92. "in the catalogue": in a list, census.

MACBETH

As hounds and greyhounds, mongrels, spaniels, curs,
Shoughs, water-rugs, and demi-wolves, are clept   94
All by the name of dogs; the valu'd file   95
Distinguishes the swift, the slow the subtle,
The housekeeper, the hunter, every one   97
According to the gift which bounteous nature
Hath in him clos'd; whereby he does receive
Particular addition, from the bill   100
That writes them all alike: and so of men.
Now, if you have a station in the file,
Not i' the worst rank of manhood, say it;
And I will put that business in your bosoms,
Whose execution takes your enemy off,   105
Grapples you to the heart and love of us,   106
Who wear our health but sickly in his life,
Which in his death were perfect.
  Second Murderer.   I am one, my liege,
Whom the vile blows and buffets of the world
Have so incens'd that I am reckless what   110
I do to spite the world.
  First Murderer.   And I another,
So weary with disasters, tugg'd with fortune,   112
That I would set my life on any chance,   113
To mend it or be rid on 't.
  Macbeth.   Both of you
Know Banquo was your enemy.
  Second Murderer.   True, my lord.
  Macbeth. So is he mine; and in such bloody   116
    distance
That every minute of his being thrusts
Against my near'st of life: and though I could   118
With bare-fac'd power sweep him from my sight
And bid my will avouch it, yet I must not,   120
For certain friends that are both his and mine,
Whose loves I may not drop, but wail his fall   122
Whom I myself struck down; and thence it is
That I to your assistance do make love,   124
Masking the business from the common eye
For sundry weighty reasons.
  Second Murderer.   We shall, my lord,
Perform what you command us.
  First Murderer.   Though our lives—   127
  Macbeth. Your spirits shine through you. Within
    this hour at most
I will advise you where to plant yourselves,
Acquaint you with the perfect spy o' the time,   130
The moment on 't; for 't must be done to-night,
And something from the palace; always thought   132
That I require a clearness: and with him—   133
To leave no rubs nor botches in the work—   134
Fleance his son, that keeps him company,
Whose absence is no less material to me
Than is his father's, must embrace the fate
Of that dark hour. Resolve yourselves apart;   138
I'll come to you anon.
  Second Murderer.   We are resolv'd, my lord.
  Macbeth. I'll call upon you straight: abide within.   140
                [*Exeunt* Murderers.
It is concluded: Banquo, thy soul's flight,
If it find heaven, must find it out to-night.   [*Exit.*

94. "Shoughs": shaggy-haired dogs. "water-rugs"; rough water dogs. "demi-wolves": dogs bred from wolves.

    "clept": called.

95. "valu'd file": a list with the worth of each.

97. "housekeeper": watchdog.

100. "Particular addition": particular title (such as hunter, etc.) "from the bill"; apart from the list.

105. "Whose . . . off": the carrying out of which gets rid of your enemy.

106. "Grapples": binds.

110. "incens'd": irritated.

112. "tugg'd with": pulled about by.

113. "set": stake. "chance": cast of the dice, hazard.

116-18. "such bloody . . . of life": The figure is that of two men dueling at close quarters (bloody distance).

118. "my near'st of life": my most vital spot.

120. "And bid . . . it": justify myself on the sole ground that it was my wish.

122. "but wail": but I must lament.

124. "That I . . . love": that I appeal to you for help.

127. "Though our lives—": Macbeth, now sure of his men, cuts them short.

130. "the perfect . . . time": the exact time when the deed should be done.

132. "something": somewhat, i.e., some distance. "always thought": it being always understood.

133. "clearness": clearness from suspicion.

134. "rubs": roughness. "botches": imperfections caused by bungling.

138. "Resolve . . . apart": make up your minds in private.

140. "straight": straightway, immediately.

MACBETH

ACT III SCENE II

Here we have the other side of the picture sketched in Scene One. Disorder and division still follow the royal couple. As soon as Macbeth, no longer engaged in his intriguing role, tries to relax, he cannot live with himself. Lady Macbeth, too, is gnawed by discontent; furthermore she is lonely. She has to send a servant after Macbeth in order to have a few words with him. She no longer knows what is happening, now that Macbeth has taken action into his own hands. Why has this division sprung up between them? What is the nature of her anxiety? Here for the first time Lady Macbeth excites pity. ("Why do you keep alone?")

She still asserts her resolute common sense, although in the face of her undefined discontent, it begins to sound a trifle hollow.

Then we learn what the new spur is that drives Macbeth into action; fear of suspicion by day, terrible dreams by night (not true sleep "that knits up the ravelled sleave of care" II,ii,37), his old repugnance working his irrepressible imagination.

In this speech two new elements make themselves felt that will grow in importance. The first is his impulse towards chaos ("Let the frame of things disjoint") as if by tearing the universe apart he could root out the source of his afflictions. (For the culmination of this, see IV,i,52-60, and IV,iii,165-73.) The second is the desire for death (ll.19-26) which affects Lady Macbeth also (ll.6-7), and has its culmination later.

See how the necessity of "beguiling the time" with a "false face" (I,v,62 and I,vii,82) is still distasteful to him.

In his last two speeches, he returns to his active role for "comfort." In expressing his new fascination for evil, the speeches gather poetic echoes of the play's symbols: the creatures of night, Hecate, beasts of prey. And yet another sinister invocation of darkness (cf. "Stars hide your fires . . ." I,iv,50) and "Come thick night" (I,v,49) affirms Macbeth's resolution.

Scene two.

(THE SAME. ANOTHER ROOM IN THE PALACE)

Enter LADY MACBETH *and a* Servant.

Lady Macbeth. Is Banquo gone from court?

Servant. Ay, madam, but returns again to-night.

Lady Macbeth. Say to the king, I would attend his 3
    leisure
For a few words.

Servant.   Madam, I will.   [*Exit.*

Lady Macbeth.   Nought's had, all's spent, 4
Where our desire is got without content: 5
'Tis safer to be that which we destroy
Than by destruction dwell in doubtful joy.

Enter MACBETH.

How now, my lord! why do you keep alone,
Of sorriest fancies your companions making, 9
Using those thoughts which should indeed have died 10
With them they think on? Things without all remedy 11
Should be without regard: what's done is done.

Macbeth. We have scotch'd the snake, not kill'd it: 13
She'll close and be herself, whilst our poor malice 14
Remains in danger of her former tooth.
But let the frame of things disjoint, both the worlds 16
    suffer,
Ere we will eat our meal in fear, and sleep
In the affliction of these terrible dreams
That shake us nightly. Better be with the dead,
Whom we, to gain our peace, have sent to peace, 20
Than on the torture of the mind to lie 21
In restless ecstasy. Duncan is in his grave; 22
After life's fitful fever he sleeps well; 23
Treason has done his worst: nor steel, nor poison, 24
Malice domestic, foreign levy, nothing 25
Can touch him further.

Lady Macbeth.   Come on;
Gentle my lord, sleek o'er your rugged looks; 27
Be bright and jovial among your guests to-night.

Macbeth. So shall I, love; and so, I pray, be you.
Let your remembrance apply to Banquo; 30
Present him eminence, both with eye and tongue: 31
Unsafe the while, that we 32
Must lave our honours in these flattering streams,
And make our faces vizards to our hearts, 34
Disguising what they are.

Lady Macbeth.   You must leave this. 35

Macbeth. O! full of scorpions is my mind, dear wife;
Thou know'st that Banquo and his Fleance lives.

Lady Macbeth. But in them nature's copy's
    not eterne. 38

Macbeth. There's comfort yet; they are assailable;
Then be thou jocund. Ere the bat hath flown 40
His cloister'd flight, ere to black Hecate's summons 41
The shard-born beetle with his drowsy hums 42
Hath rung night's yawning peal, there shall be done
A deed of dreadful note.

Lady Macbeth.   What's to be done? 44

3-4. "I would . . . few words": I should like to speak to him when he is at his leisure.

4. "Nought's had": We have gained nothing.

5. "content": happiness.

9. "sorriest fancies": most gloomy and despicable thoughts.

10. "Using": keeping in your mind.

11. "without all": beyond all.

13. "scotch'd": slashed, gashed.

14. "close": come together.

14-15. "whilst our . . . tooth": while we with our feeble enmity revealed will remain in as much danger as ever from its still venomous fangs.

16. "let the . . . disjoint": let the whole structure of the universe fall apart.

20. "our peace": our peace of mind.

21-2. "Than on . . . ecstasy": the mind is compared to a rack on which a prisoner is tortured.

22. "ecstasy": frenzy.

23. "life's fitful fever": Life seems to Macbeth a tormenting malarial fever.

24. "his": its.

25. "foreign levy": invasion.

27. "Gentle my lord": my gentle lord.

30. "Let . . . Banquo": Remember to show particular attention to Banquo.

31. "Present him eminence": do him special honors.

32-3. "Unsafe . . . streams": while they wash ("lave") away suspicions of their honor with flattery, they themselves are unsafe.

34. "vizards": masks.

35. "this": such wild remarks.

38. "not eterne": Nature had granted them a temporary lease of life. She probably merely reminds him that they must some day die a natural death.

40. "jocund": joyful.

41. "cloister'd": in belfries and cloisters—in darkness and solitude.

42. "shard": a fragment of pottery. The covering of a beetle's wings are crisp and hard.

44. "of dreadful note": dreadful to be known.

ACT III SCENE III

Scenes like this, not literature, but spectacle, remind us of the theatrical reality of the play. A drama seen, no matter how long-winded the speeches, is always less wordy than a drama read, because one is always watching just as much as listening, and the actor mimes his meaning as well as mouthing it. The reader, knowing his disadvantage, must always picture the action. The really acute reader of a play is the producer-director of his own ideal performance as he reads.

Macbeth's growing suspicion appears in his sending a third murderer to check on the other two. Where does such a process end?

Macbeth. Be innocent of the knowledge, dearest chuck,   45
Till thou applaud the deed. Come, seeling night,   46
Scarf up the tender eye of pitiful day,   47
And with thy bloody and invisible hand
Cancel and tear to pieces that great bond   49
Which keeps me pale! Light thickens, and the crow
Makes wing to the rooky wood;   51
Good things of day begin to droop and drowse,
Whiles night's black agents to their preys do rouse.   53
Thou marvell'st at my words: but hold thee still;
Things bad begun make strong themselves by ill:
So, prithee, go with me.   [*Exeunt.* 56

Scene three.

(THE SAME. A PARK WITH A ROAD LEADING TO THE PALACE)

Enter three Murderers.

First Murderer. But who did bid thee join with us? 1
Third Murderer.   Macbeth.
Second Murderer. He needs not our mistrust, since he delivers   2
Our offices and what we have to do   3
To the direction just.
First Murderer.   Then stand with us. 4
The west yet glimmers with some streaks of day:
Now spurs the lated traveller apace   6
To gain the timely inn; and near approaches   7
The subject of our watch.
Third Murderer.   Hark! I hear horses.
Banquo. [*Within.*] Give us a light there, ho!
Second Murderer.   Then 'tis he: the rest 9
That are within the note of expectation   10
Already are i' the court.
First Murderer.   His horses go about. 11
Third Murderer. Almost a mile; but he does usually,
So all men do, from hence to the palace gate
Make it their walk.
    Enter BANQUO *and* FLEANCE, *with a torch.*
Second Murderer. A light, a light!
Third Murderer.   'Tis he.
First Murderer. Stand to 't.
Banquo. It will be rain to-night.
First Murderer.   Let it come down. 16
           [*They set upon* BANQUO.
Banquo. O, treachery! Fly, good Fleance, fly, fly, fly!
Thou mayst revenge. O slave!
        [*Dies.* FLEANCE *escapes.*
Third Murderer. Who did strike out the light?
First Murderer.   Was 't not the way?
Third Murderer. There's but one down; the son is fled.
Second Murderer.   We have lost
Best half of our affair.
First Murderer. Well, let's away, and say how much is done.   [*Exeunt.*

45. "chuck": chicken, a term of endearment.
46. "seeling": to seel is to sew up a falcon's eyelids with silk—to tame it.
47. "Scarf up": blindfold, as with a scarf.
49. "bond": the prophecy by which Fate has bound itself to give the throne to Banquo's descendants.
51. "rooky"; the resort of rooks or crows.
53. "agents": all evil beings that act by night, e.g., wild beasts, murderers, witches, etc.
56. "go with me": come with me. Macbeth gives her his hand to lead her off the stage.

1. We hear only the end of the dialogue.

2. "delivers": reports.

3. "offices": duties.

4. "To the direction just": exactly according to our instructions.

6. "lated": belated.

7. "To gain the timely inn": to reach the inn in good time (before it is quite dark).

9. "Give . . . ho": a call to a servant of the palace to light their way with a torch.

10. "within . . . expectation": in the list of expected guests.

11. "His horses go about": Fleance has taken the torch and the servant has taken the horses around to the rear of the castle. Macbeth has arranged that the murder would take place after Banquo and Fleance have dismounted. This allows the use of fewer assailants. It incidentally avoids bringing horses on stage.

16. "It will rain to-night": This casual remark shows that Banquo is off his guard, and informs the audience of the cloudy sky—in harmony with murder.

MACBETH

With its elaborate picture of false order collapsing into disorder, this famous scene is a notable disaster for Macbeth; the end of his dream of security. For this scene Shakespeare rearranged Holinshed's story in which Banquo was slain after the banquet on his way home.

There is some problem in staging this scene to make it clear which speeches are supposed to be heard by whom. To get the banquet out onto their uncurtained stage, it would have been set up behind the curtains of the inner stage. Then at the proper moment, the curtains opened, the whole banquet would be neatly carried forward.

"Degrees," "humble host," "her state" are all references to the ceremony of state banquets (thus an evocation of order) at which guests were placed at the table according to their social rank. Macbeth has decided to remain humbly in the midst of them rather than take his state (i.e., place at the head of the table beside Lady Macbeth). He intends, that is, to befriend his thanes by means of false heartiness.

The escape of Fleance is Macbeth's first intimation that all is not according to plan. It has a sinister ring and indicates that the witches's and their master are not tricked.

Lines 21-3 give a glimpse of his hopes. They are represented by images of solidity relying on natural order, and bathed in air like that which nimbly and sweetly cased his castle when Duncan came there (cf. "We have scotch'd the snake . . ." [III,ii,13]). But the image as first used applies to more than merely Banquo.

The ghost should be quite terrible, bleeding copiously, because folklore had it that ghosts would bleed if in the presence of their killer. Macbeth, in the act of wishing for Banquo, must have his back to the ghost. Some of the lords should be so placed that it is clear as quickly as possible that they do not see it.

The dramatic delay before Macbeth can single out and recognize the ghost, natural and effective as it is, also provides us with a demonstration that the ghost is not, like the dagger, a hallucination. This difference is further represented in the fact that the audience sees the ghost but not the dagger. Yet it cannot be a real ghost, since neither the lords nor Lady Macbeth see it. King James

---

Scene four.

(THE SAME. A ROOM OF STATE IN THE PALACE)

A Banquet prepared. Enter MACBETH, LADY MACBETH, ROSS, LENNOX, Lords, *and* Attendants

Macbeth. You know your own degrees; sit down: at   1
first and last,
The hearty welcome.
Lords.   Thanks to your majesty.
Macbeth. Ourself will mingle with society   3
And play the humble host.
Our hostess keeps her state, but in best time   5
We will require her welcome.
Lady Macbeth. Pronounce it for me, sir, to all our
friends;
For my heart speaks they are welcome.   8

Enter First Murderer, *to the door.*

Macbeth. See, they encounter thee with their hearts'   9
thanks;
Both sides are even: here I'll sit i' the midst:
Be large in mirth; anon, we'll drink a measure   11
The table round. [*Approaching the door.*] There's
blood upon thy face.
Murderer. 'Tis Banquo's, then.
Macbeth. 'Tis better thee without than he within.   14
Is he dispatch'd?
Murderer. My lord, his throat is cut; that I did for
him.
Macbeth. Thou art the best o' the cut-throats; yet
he's good
That did the like for Fleance: if thou didst it,
Thou art the nonpareil.
Murderer.   Most royal sir,   19
Fleance is 'scap'd.
Macbeth. Then comes my fit again: I had else been
perfect;   21
Whole as the marble, founded as the rock,   22
As broad and general as the casing air: 23
But now I am cabin'd, cribb'd, confined, bound in   24
To saucy doubts and fears. But Banquo's safe?   25
Murderer. Ay, my good lord; safe in a ditch he
bides,
With twenty trenched gashes on his head,   27
The least a death to nature.
Macbeth.   Thanks for that.
There the grown serpent lies: the worm that's fled   29
Hath nature that in time will venom breed,
No teeth for the present. Get thee gone; to-morrow
We'll hear ourselves again.   [*Exit* Murderer.
Lady Macbeth.   My royal lord,   32
You do not give the cheer: the feast is sold   33
That is not often vouch'd, while 'tis a-making,
'Tis given with welcome: to feed were best at home;   35
From thence, the sauce to meat is ceremony;
Meeting were bare without it.
Macbeth.   Sweet remembrancer!   37

1. "degrees": ranks.
"at first and last": once and for all.

3. "Ourself": it is customary for royalty to use the plural pronoun, as representing the whole country (cf. "gracious England," IV,iii,189).

5-6. "Our hostess . . . her welcome": our hostess will keep her chair of state, but when the proper moment comes ("in best time") we will call on her to make us welcome.

8. The first three speeches of the King and Queen each end with welcome, which is thus strongly emphasized.

9. "encounter": respond to.

11. "large": lavish, abundant.
"measure": a large goblet.

14. "'Tis . . . within": it's better that the blood is on the outside of your face than inside Banquo's body.

19. "nonpareil": without equal.

21. "my fit": my fit of feverous anxiety.
"perfect": completely secure.

22. "founded": firmly established.

23. "broad and general": free and unconfined.
"casing": all-embracing.

24. "cabin'd, cribb'd": shut up in a cabin, a stall.

25. "To saucy": with insolent.

27. "trenched": deep-cut.

29. "worm": serpent.

32. "hear ourselves": talk by ourselves.

33. "give the cheer": make your guests feel welcome.

33-5. "the feast . . . welcome": Unless guests are made welcome, it is like a feast for which they are paying.

35. "to feed . . . home": as for mere eating one could do it better at home.

37. "remembrancer": one who reminds one of his duty.

MACBETH

ACT III SCENE IV

in DAEMONOLOGIE provides us with an explanation designed to reconcile ghosts with protestant theology. They were apparitions of the devil allowed by God as a punishment to the guilty or the faithless.

"Which of you have done this?" His first thought seems to be that the corpse has been brought in. Then it moves.

From "Are you a man?" (l.58) down to line 83 is between Macbeth and his wife, and not heard by the thanes. The remainder of the scene is heard by all.

Lady Macbeth's reference to the dagger scene is clear. She also reiterates her rejection of imagination as childish unreality in the same metaphor of a painting (cf. "the sleeping and the dead/are but as pictures: 'tis the eye of childhood/ That fears a painted devil" [II,ii,54-6]).

Compare "twenty mortal murders" (l.81) to the "twenty trenched gashes" in line 27.

Now good digestion wait on appetite,   38
And health on both!

Lennox.   May it please your highness sit?
[*The Ghost of* BANQUO *enters, and sits in* MACBETH's *place.*

Macbeth. Here had we now our country's honour   40
    roof'd,
Were the grac'd person of our Banquo present;
Who may I rather challenge for unkindness   42
Than pity for mischance!

Ross.   His absence, sir,
Lays blame upon his promise. Please 't your highness
To grace us with your royal company.   45

Macbeth. The table's full.

Lennox.   Here is a place reserv'd, sir.

Macbeth. Where?

Lennox. Here, my good lord. What is 't that moves   48
    your highness?

Macbeth. Which of you have done this?

Lords.   What, my good lord?

Macbeth. Thou canst not say I did it: never shake
Thy gory locks at me.   51

Ross. Gentlemen, rise; his highness is not well.

Lady Macbeth. Sit, worthy friends: my lord is often
    thus,
And hath been from his youth: pray you, keep seat;
The fit is momentary; upon a thought   55
He will again be well. If much you note him,
You shall offend him and extend his passion:
Feed, and regard him not. Are you a man?   58

Macbeth. Ay, and a bold one, that dare look on that
Which might appal the devil.

Lady Macbeth.   O proper stuff!   60
This is the very painting of your fear;   61
This is the air-drawn dagger which, you said,
Led you to Duncan. O! these flaws and starts—   63
Impostors to true fear—would well become   64
A woman's story at a winter's fire,
Authoriz'd by her grandam. Shame itself!   66
Why do you make such faces? When all's done,
You look but on a stool.

Macbeth. Prithee, see there! behold! look! lo!
    how say you?   69
Why, what care I? If thou canst nod, speak too.
If charnel-houses and our graves must send   71
Those that we bury back, our monuments   72
Shall be the maws of kites.   [*Ghost disappears.*   73

Lady Macbeth. What! quite unmann'd in folly?

Macbeth. If I stand here, I saw him.

Lady Macbeth.   Fie, for shame!

Macbeth. Blood hath been shed ere now, i' the olden
    time,
Ere human statute purg'd the gentle weal;   76
Ay, and since too, murders have been perform'd   77
Too terrible for the ear: the times have been,
That, when the brains were out, the man would die,
And there an end; but now they rise again,
With twenty mortal murders on their crowns,   81
And push us from our stools: this is more strange
Than such a murder is.

---

38. "wait on ": attend, accompany.

40. "had we . . . roof'd": we should now have all the noblest men of Scotland under one roof.

42-3. "Who may . . . mischance": Macbeth intends to compliment Banquo by saying that the pain of being without him outweighs the anxiety as to what might have happened to delay him.

45. "grace": honor.

48. "moves": disturbs.

51. "gory locks": The hair of the apparition is matted with blood from the "twenty trenched gashes."

55. "upon a thought": in a moment.

58. "Feed." The guests apply themselves to the banquet and do not hear what follows.

60. "O proper stuff": A fine thing this!

61. "painting of your fear": imaginary vision prompted by fear.

63. "flaws": outbursts. .

64. "to": in comparison with.

66. "Authoriz'd": vouched for

69-73. During the utterance of these lines, the ghost rises, glares fixedly at Macbeth, nods its head, and moves toward the back of the stage.

71. "charnel-houses": houses or vaults used as storehouses for bones found while digging new graves.

72-3. "our monuments . . . kites": if the dead are thrown out to be devoured by birds of prey such as kites, their only monuments will be kites's bellies.

76. "Ere . . . weal": before civilizing laws cleansed society of savagery and made it gentle.

77. "since too": since then too.

81. "twenty . . . crowns": an echo of the murderer's words in lines 27, 28. "mortal murders": murderous wounds.

MACBETH

ACT III SCENE IV

Macbeth's reassumed heartiness seems ghastly now. The irony of the ghost's return when called for is complex. Banquo certainly is not failing the feast (see III,i, 28-9).

Compare these two remarks by Macbeth: "What man dare I dare" (l.99) and "I dare do all that may become a man" (I,vii,46).

"The order of your going" (l.119) is another reference to formal etiquette. The leave-taking should be performed with ceremony according to order of rank. But the banquet is disordered even as Macbeth's plans are.

Line 122 is reminiscent of "Bloody instructions" which "return To plague the inventor" (I,vii, 9-10).

The events of the evening have awakened a superstitious fear of discovery through supernatural agencies, as well they might. He accords full authority again to the witches. In the mean time Macduff is next on the list, and he turns back to his role of intriguer. How many must he kill now to banish suspicion?

Lady Macbeth. My worthy lord,	83

Your noble friends do lack you.

Macbeth. I do forget.	84

Do not muse at me, my most worthy friends;   85
I have a strange infirmity, which is nothing
To those that know me. Come, love and health to all;
Then, I'll sit down. Give me some wine; fill full.
I drink to the general joy of the whole table.
And to our dear friend Banquo, whom we miss;   90
Would he were here! to all, and him, we thirst,
And all to all.

Lords. Our duties, and the pledge.	92

Re-enter Ghost

  Macbeth. Avaunt! and quit my sight! Let the earth
    hide thee!
Thy bones are marrowless, thy blood is cold;
Thou hast no speculation in those eyes   95
Which thou dost glare with.

Lady Macbeth. Think of this, good peers,	

But as a thing of custom: 'tis no other;   97
Only it spoils the pleasure of the time.
  Macbeth. What man dare, *I* dare:
Approach thou like the rugged Russian bear,
The arm'd rhinoceros, or the Hyrcan tiger;   101
Take any shape but that, and my firm nerves
Shall never tremble: or be alive again,
And dare me to the desert with thy sword;   104
If trembling I inhabit then, protest me   105
The baby of a girl. Hence, horrible shadow!
Unreal mockery, hence!   [*Ghost vanishes.*

Why, so; being gone,	107

I am a man again. Pray you, sit still.   108
  Lady Macbeth. You have displac'd the mirth, broke
    the good meeting,
With most admir'd disorder.

Macbeth. Can such things be	110

And overcome us like a summer's cloud,   111
Without our special wonder? You make me strange   112
Even to the disposition that I owe,   113
When now I think you can behold such sights,
And keep the natural ruby of your cheeks,
When mine are blanch'd with fear.

Ross. What sights, my lord?	

  Lady Macbeth. I pray you, speak not; he grows
    worse and worse;
Question enrages him. At once, good-night;   118
Stand not upon the order of your going,   119
But go at once.
  Lennox.   Good-night; and better health
Attend his majesty!
  Lady Macbeth.   A kind good-night to all!
              [*Exeunt* Lords *and* Attendants.
  Macbeth. It will have blood, they say; blood will
    have blood:
Stones have been known to move and trees to   123
    speak;
Augures and understand relations have   124
By maggot-pies and choughs and rooks brought   125
    forth
The secret'st man of blood. What is the night?

83. "My worthy lord" etc.: The guests hear the following speeches.

84. "lack you": miss your company.

85. "muse": wonder, be astonished.

90-1. Macbeth has persuaded himself that the ghost was an illusion. With superb hardihood, he repeats his wish that Banquo were present. Instantly the ghost accepts the challenge.

92. "And all to all": let everyone drink to everyone else.
"Our duties . . . pledge": Our toast is—homage to your king and health to all and to Banquo.

95. "speculation": intelligent sight. The ghost's eyes are fixed in a glassy stare.

97. "no other": nothing else.

101. "arm'd": referring either to the thick hide or to the tusks.
"Hyrcan": Hyrcania was a district south of the Caspian Sea. Their tigers were represented in classical literature as being particularly fierce.

104. "to the desert": to some solitary place for a duel without witnesses.

105. "inhabit": give lodging to.

105-6. "protest . . . a girl": "declares me the child of a very young mother, i.e., timid weakling.

107. "being gone": now that it is gone.

108. "Pray . . . still": The guests are rising in horrified amazement.

110. "With . . . disorder": by an amazing fit of distraction.

111-12. "overcome . . . wonder": come over us as suddenly as a cloud in summer, yet excite no more surprise than such a cloud.

112-13. "You . . . owe": You make me feel that I do not know my own nature ("disposition"), which I had supposed to be that of a brave man.

113. "owe": own.

118. "At . . . night": I bid you all a hasty goodnight in a body.

119. "Stand . . . going": Under ordinary circumstances the nobles would depart ceremoniously, in the order of their rank as they leave the hall.

123. "Stones . . . move": so as to reveal the body that the murderer had hidden.

124. "Augures": auguries, signs from the flight of birds.

125. "By": by means of.
"maggot-pies": magpies.
"choughs": a kind of crow.

MACBETH

ACT III SCENE V

Scholars agree that this scene, so out of character with the rest, so dramatically pointless, was added to the play some time after 1609 by Thomas Middleton, in order to cater to the current taste for spectacular ballets, and to demonstrate the mechanical resources of their new indoor theater. The light, sophisticated tone, classical imagery, and iambic meter (i.e., the lines begin with an unstressed syllable) of the verse are not a bit like the grotesque, ballad-like, trochaic meter of Shakespeare's witches.

The song, not printed with the text, appeared originally (together with the one in IV,i) in Middleton's unsuccessful play, THE WITCH. As you can see, it would occupy more than half the scene's length in a performance, and ridiculously detract from the tragedy. Here it is with stage directions in brackets:

(Song — in the air)
Come away: Come away:
Hecate, Hecate, Come away.
(Hecate sings)
I come, I come, I come, I come,
With all the speed I may,
With all the speed I may,
Where's Stadlin?/(Voice in the air) Here.
Where's Puckle?/ (Voice in the air) Here.
(In the air)
And Hoppo too,/ and Hellwaine too
We lack but you;/ we lack but you;
Come away. Make up the count
(Hecate)
I will but noynt and then I mount.
(above) (a spirit like a cat descends in a cloud)
There's one comes down to fetch his dues
A kiss, a coll, a sip of blood
And why thou stayest so long
I muse, I muse.
Since the air's so sweet and good.
(Hecate)
Oh, are thou come?
What news: what news
(the spirit)
Either come, or else
Refuse: Refuse.
(Hecate speaks her closing lines; then ascends on a wire and disappears through the ceiling, while the following is sung.)
Now I go, now I fly,
Malkin my sweet spirit and I.
To ride in the air
Oh what a daintie pleasure 'tis
When the moon shines fair
And sing and dance and toy and kiss
Over woods, high rocks and mountains
Over seas, our Mistress Fountains,
Over steep towers and turrets

Lady Macbeth. Almost at odds with morning, which is which.
Macbeth. How sayst thou, that Macduff denies his person   128
At our great bidding?
Lady Macbeth.   Did you send to him, sir?
Macbeth. I hear it by the way; but I will send.   130
There's not a one of them but in his house   131
I keep a servant fee'd. I will to-morrow—
And betimes I will—to the weird sisters: 133
More shall they speak; for now I am bent to know,   134
By the worst means, the worst. For mine own good   135
All causes shall give way: I am in blood   136
Stepp'd in so far, that, should I wade no more,
Returning were as tedious as go o'er.
Strange things I have in head that will to hand.   139
Which must be acted ere they may be scann'd.   140
Lady Macbeth. You lack the season of all natures, sleep.   141
Macbeth. Come, we'll to sleep. My strange and self-abuse   142
Is the initiate fear that wants hard use: 143
We are yet but young in deed.   [*Exeunt.*

Scene five.

(A HEATH)

Thunder. Enter the three witches, meeting HECATE.

First Witch. Why, how now, Hecate! you look angerly.   1
Hecate. Have I not reason, beldams as you are,   2
Saucy and overbold? How did you dare
To trade and traffic with Macbeth
In riddles and affairs of death;
And I, the mistress of your charms,
The close contriver of all harms,   7
Was never call'd to bear my part,
Or show the glory of our art?
And, which is worse, all you have done
Hath been but for a wayward son,   11
Spiteful and wrathful; who, as others do,
Loves for his own ends, not for you.   13
But make amends now: get you gone,
And at the pit of Acheron   15
Meet me i' the morning: thither he
Will come to know his destiny:
Your vessels and your spells provide,
Your charms and every thing beside.
I am for the air; this night I'll spend
Unto a dismal and a fatal end: 21
Great business must be wrought ere noon:
Upon the corner of the moon
There hangs a vaporous drop profound;   24
I'll catch it ere it come to ground:
And that distill'd by magic sleights   26
Shall raise such artificial sprites   27

---

128. "How . . . that": what do you say to the fact that.

130. "by the way": in the ordinary course of affairs.

131. Macbeth explains that the report has come from one of his spies in Macduff's household.

133. "betimes": soon, without delay.

134. "bent": determined.

135. "By": even by. Macbeth no longer doubts that the Weird Sisters are powers of evil.

136. "All causes": all considerations, including scruples about seeking help from evil powers.

139. "will to hand": are bound to be executed.

140. "ere . . . scann'd": before I pause to consider them.

141. "the season": the preservative.

142. "My . . . self-abuse": my strange self-deception. He persuades himself that the ghost was an illusion.

143. "the initiate fear": fear felt by a beginner.
"wants": lacks.
"hard use": practice that hardens one.

This scene is an interpolation not written by Shakespeare. See commentary.

1. "angerly": angrily.

2. "beldams": hags.

7. "close": secret.
"of all harms": of the evil deeds

11. "a wayward son": indicating that Macbeth is unfaithful to the evil spirits whose lead he followed.

13. "Loves": Macbeth has never professed to love the sisters or to be a devotee of magic. The distinction here is between a lover of evil and one who merely makes use of an evil means. Macbeth is not yet the former.

15. "the pit of Acheron": It is certainly not to Acheron (a mythical river of the infernal regions) that Macbeth goes to find the witches but to a Scottish cavern.

21. "dismal": disastrous.

24. "a . . . profound": a drop of condensed vapor, deep-hanging, pear-shaped, and ready to fall. This moon-vapor is nowhere mentioned in the later scene around the witches's cauldron.

26. "sleights": sacred arts.

27. "artificial sprites": spirits produced by magic.

MACBETH

ACT III SCENE V

We fly by night, 'mongst troops of
  sprites.
No ring of bells to our ears sounds
No howls of wolves, no yelps of
  hounds,
No, not the noise of waters breech
Or cannon's throat our height can
  reach.
(Repeat last four lines till out of
  sight.)

ACT III SCENE VI

Scene Six resembles II,iv, (the old man scene), devoted as it is to the state of affairs as seen by observers, rather than participants.

The conscious irony of Lennox's opening speech is eloquent of the bitter judgment of the thanes since the banquet. The amount of knowledge they possess (more than Macbeth for all his spy systems [see III,iv,131-2]). indicates considerable wary activity on their own part.

Malcolm's hereditary right to the throne refers to the operation of the new law (see I,iv and commentary) of the times, but at the same time chimes in with Elizabethan popular feeling, and with King James's theories of Divine Right.

Mention of pious Edward introduces yet another symbolic contrast between good/order and evil/disorder, which is more fully developed in IV,iii. Here it is reinforced by reference to "grace" "holiness," "Him above," "angel," and "blessing."

Line 34 suggests that, just as Macbeth's evil has darkened his country, his sleeplessness also has spread.

Though dramatically well-placed here so that we know of the reaction against Macbeth before we see him meet the witches, there is evidence that this scene was written to go later in the play. Lines 37-9 suggest that Macbeth knows of Macduff's flight to England, and already prepares his forces, although he does not hear the news of Macduff's departure officially until IV,i,142. Yet Lennox asks where Macduff is. If he appears in this scene, someone else must be with Macbeth in IV,i. There is no sure solution to this problem of abridgement and rearrangement in the text of MACBETH.

As by the strength of their illusion
Shall draw him on to his confusion:　　29
He shall spurn fate, scorn death, and bear
His hopes 'bove wisdom, grace, and fear;　　31
And you all know, security　　32
Is mortals' chiefest enemy.
　　　　[*Song within*, 'Come away, come away,' &c　33
Hark! I am call'd; my little spirit, see,
Sits in a foggy cloud, and stays for me.　　[*Exit.*
First Witch. Come, let's make haste; she'll soon
　　be back again.　　　　　　　　[*Exeunt.*

Scene six.

(FORRES. A ROOM IN THE PALACE)
Enter LENNOX *and another* LORD.

Lennox. My former speeches have but hit your　　1
　　thoughts,
Which can interpret further: only, I say,　　2
Things have been strangely borne. The gracious　　3
　　Duncan
Was pitied of Macbeth: marry, he was dead:　　4
And the right-valiant Banquo walk'd too late;
Whom, you may say, if 't please you, Fleance kill'd　　6
For Fleance fled: men must not walk too late.
Who cannot want the thought how monstrous
It was for Malcolm and for Donalbain
To kill their gracious father? damned fact!　　10
How it did grieve Macbeth! did he not straight　　11
In pious rage the two delinquents tear,
That were the slaves of drink and thralls of sleep?　　13
Was not that nobly done? Ay, and wisely too;
For 'twould have anger'd any heart alive
To hear the men deny 't. So that, I say,　　16
He has borne all things well; and I do think
That, had he Duncan's sons under his key,—
As an 't please heaven, he shall not,—they
　　should find　　19
What 'twere to kill a father; so should Fleance.
But, peace! for from broad words, and 'cause he fail'd　　21
His presence at the tyrant's feast, I hear
Macduff lives in disgrace. Sir, can you tell
Where he bestows himself?
　　Lord. 　　　　　　The son of Duncan,　　24
From whom this tyrant holds the due of birth,　　25
Lives in the English court, and is receiv'd
Of the most pious Edward with such grace　　27
That the malevolence of fortune nothing
Takes from his high respect. Thither Macduff　　29
Is gone to pray the holy king, upon his aid　　30
To wake Northumberland and war-like Siward:　　31
That, by the help of these—with him above
To ratify the work—we may again
Give to our tables meat, sleep to our nights,　　34
Free from our feasts and banquets bloody knives,
Do faithful homage and receive free honours;　　36
All which we pine for now. And this report　　37

43

29. "confusion": destruction, ruin.

31. "grace": goodness, virtue.

32. "security": a sense of security which makes mortals overbold.

33. "Come away": This song appears in full in a play by Middleton called THE WITCH. It was probably written by Middleton and used in productions of MACBETH after Shakespreare left the theater.

In the interval between Scenes iv and vi Macbeth has carried out his purpose of summoning Macduff and has received a curt refusal.

1. "My former speeches": Lennox has been feeling out this man before.

2. "Which . . . further": Your mind can easily draw its own conclusions from the hints.

3. "strangely borne": oddly managed by Macbeth.

4. "marry": an exclamation.

6-7. "Whom . . . fled": ironic argument. Macbeth's sole proof of Duncan's sons's guilt is their flight.

10. "fact": evil deed, crime.

11. "did . . . straight" etc.: ironic remark. Macbeth's real motive (to keep the chamberlains from talking) is plainly hinted in line 16.

13. "the slaves of drink": Lennox insinuates that the grooms could not have killed Duncan, for they had slept in a drunken stupor all night.

16-17. "So that . . . well": The upshot of the whole matter is that Macbeth has managed everything wisely.

19. "should find": would be sure to find; ironic.

21. "from broad words": because of too free or unguarded expressions.

24. "bestows himself": has taken refuge.

25. "holds": withholds.
"due of birth": birthright.

27. "Of": by.
"grace": favor.

"Edward": Edward the Confessor.

29. "his high respect": the high regard in which he is held.

30. "upon his aid": for his assistance.

31. "wake": call to arms.
"Northumberland": the people of that region.
"Siward": Earl of Northumberland.

34. "meat": food.

36. "faithful": sincere.

37. "this report": of the favor with which Malcolm is treated.

MACBETH

Hath so exasperate the king that he 38
Prepares for some attempt of war.
    Lennox.   Sent he to Macduff?
    Lord. He did: and with an absolute, 'Sir, not I,'
The cloudy messenger turns me his back, 41
And hums, as who should say, 'You'll rue the time 42
That clogs me with this answer.'
    Lennox.   And that well might 43
Advise him to a caution to hold what distance
His wisdom can provide. Some holy angel
Fly to the court of England and unfold 46
His message ere he come, that a swift blessing
May soon return to this our suffering country
Under a hand accurs'd!
    Lord.   I'll send my prayers with him!
                          [Exeunt.

38. "exasperate": exasperated.

41. "cloudy": frowning, gloomy.

42. "hums": a surly murmuring sound.

43. "clogs": stuffs.

46. "unfold": disclose, reveal.

44

MACBETH

Details of the accessories of witchcraft may be found in many sources. The following details relevant to the present charm were recorded by King James:

(News from Scotland) "Agnis Tompson confessed that she took a black toad and did hang the same up by the heels, three days, and collected the venom as it dropped and fell from it,—in an oyster shell, and kept the same venom close covered (to be used in a spell against King James)," and later in her confession, "She took a cat and christened it, and afterwards bound to each part of the cat the chiefest parts of a dead man, and several joints of his body."

In the first three lines the witches listen to the voices of their attendant spirits, who command them.

Again (see III,v, and commentary) Hecate's appearance serves no purpose except to provide for the song and dance spectacle. This time she is left on the stage with nothing to do until the witches's dance after line 132. Here is Middleton's second song as it would have been sung with the play at Blackfriars theater:

Black Spirits and white: Red spirits and gray,

Mingle, mingle, mingle, you that mingle may.

Titty, Tiffin: keep it stiff in

Firedrake, Puckey, make it lucky Liand, Robin,/ you must bob in.

Round, around, around,/ about, about.

All ill come running in,/ all good keep out.

(1st witch) Here's the blood of a bat.

(Hecate) Put in that: Oh put in that.

(2nd witch) Here's Libbard's bane
(Hecate) Put in again

(1st witch) The juice of toad: the oil of adder

(2nd witch) Those will make the yonker madder

(3rd witch) Hey, here's three ounces of a red-haired wench.

(Hecate) Put in: There's all, and rid the stench.

(All together) Round, around, around, about, about.

All ill come running in, all good keep out.

ACT FOUR, scene one.

(A Cavern. In the middle, a boiling Cauldron.)

Thunder. Enter the three Witches.

First Witch.	Thrice the brinded cat hath mew'd.	1
Second Witch.	Thrice and once the hedge-pig whin'd.	2
Third Witch.	Harpier cries: 'Tis time, 'tis time.	3
First Witch.	Round about the cauldron go;	
	In the poison'd entrails throw.	
	Toad, that under cold stone	6
	Days and nights hast thirty-one	
	Swelter'd venom sleeping got,	8
	Boil thou first i' the charmed pot.	
All.	Double, double toil and trouble;	
	Fire burn and cauldron bubble.	
Second Witch.	Fillet of a fenny snake,	12
	In the cauldron boil and bake;	
	Eye of newt, and toe of frog,	14
	Wool of bat, and tongue of dog,	
	Adder's fork, and blind-worm's sting,	16
	Lizard's leg, and howlet's wing,	17
	For a charm of powerful trouble,	
	Like a hell-broth boil and bubble.	
All.	Double, double toil and trouble;	
	Fire burn and cauldron bubble.	
Third Witch.	Scale of dragon, tooth of wolf,	
	Witches' mummy, maw and gulf	23
	Of the ravin'd salt-sea shark,	24
	Root of hemlock digg'd i' the dark,	25
	Liver of blaspheming Jew,	
	Gall of goat, and slips of yew	27
	Sliver'd in the moon's eclipse,	
	Nose of Turk, and Tartar's lips,	
	Finger of birth-strangled babe	30
	Ditch-deliver'd by a drab,	
	Make the gruel thick and slab:	32
	Add there to a tiger's chaudron,	33
	For the ingredients of our cauldron.	
All.	Double, double toil and trouble;	
	Fire burn and cauldron bubble.	
Second Witch.	Cool it with a baboon's blood,	
	Then the charm is firm and good.	

Enter HECATE.

Hecate.	O! well done! I commend your pains,	39
	And every one shall share i' the games.	
	And now about the cauldron sing,	
	Like elves and fairies in a ring,	
	Enchanting all that you put in.	
	[*Music and a song,* 'Black Spirits,' &c	43
Second Witch.	By the pricking of my thumbs,	
	Something wicked this way comes.	
	Open, locks,	46
	Whoever knocks.	

1. "brinded": striped, streaked, brindled.

2. "hedge-pig": hedgehog.

3. "Harpier": an attendant demon.

6. "cold": the "o" is prolonged with a change of pitch to give the effect of two syllables.

8. "Swelter'd": coming out in drops (like sweat).

12. "Fillet": strip or slice
"fenny": living in a bog, marsh.

14. "newt": meaning forked-tongue.

16. "Adder's fork": meaning forked-tongue.
"blind-worm": small, snake-like lizard erroneously supposed to be sightless and venomous.

17. "howlet": owlet.

23. "Witches' mummy": bits of Egyptian mummy, or what passed for it (often powdered) . . . were traditional parts of these spells.
"maw and gulf": stomach and gullet.

24. "ravin'd": ravenous.

25. "hemlock": a poisonous herb.

27. "yew": evergreen found in church yards (poisonous).

30. "birth-strangled": hence unbaptized.

32. "slab": slimy.

33. "chaudron": insides, entrails.

39-43. Hecate's speech is by the same hand as Act III Scene v. The comparison with elves and fairies is quite out of order.

43. "Black Spirits": This song also occurs in Middleton's THE WITCH.

46. "Open, locks": This does not imply that the Sisters are in a locked room rather than a cave. It is a formula of admission, releasing any spells that prevent the entrance of intruders.

MACBETH

ACT IV SCENE 1

The urgency of Macbeth's need to know what is in store is expressed in the strongest of his expressions of disregard for order. This time he evokes a strong picture of chaos. The following passage translated from Seneca's THYESTES (translated into English and published in 1560, 1566, 1578, 1581) is analogous to it. (Seneca is an important source for Elizabethan tragic method.) "Our hearts tremble . . . lest the whole universe collapse in fragments in the general ruin, lest chaos should come again and overwhelm both gods and men (cf. "both the worlds suffer"), and earth and sea be engulfed with the wandering planets scattered over the sky."

Palaces and pyramids (see note) are, of course, symbolic of state and church.

King Kenneth II (Duncan's predecessor) had made a law regarding such sows, which Holinshed reports thus: "If a sow eat her pigs, let her be stoned to death and buried, so that no man eat of her flesh." But why should they be stoned unless unnatural animals were hated and feared as well as considered inedible.

According to DAEMONOLOGIE these apparitions would be the devil appearing in various forms.

Compare the mocking and commanding tones of the witches here with the respectful grandeur of I,iii. It is a measure of his degradation that these creatures can treat him so.

THE PROPHECIES: (From Holinshed) "Macbeth had learned of certain wizards, in whose words he put great confidence (because of the three sisters) how that he ought to take heed of Macduff, who in time to come should seek to destroy him. And surely hereupon had he put Macduff to death, but that a certain witch whom he had in great trust told that he should never be slain with man born of any woman, nor vanquished till the wood of Birnham came to the castle of Dunsinane. . . . This vain hope caused him to do many outrageous things to the grievous oppression of his subjects."

Notice how Macbeth, in spite of his impulses to destroy all order when he lashes out against his torment, unconsciously here and elsewhere relies upon the firm order of nature: "Who can bid the tree unfix his earthbound root?" and see also, "Whole as the marble, founded as the rock" (III,iv,22).

The sinking of the cauldron would be by means of a trapdoor

Enter MACBETH.

Macbeth. How now, you secret, black, and
   midnight hags!
What is 't you do?
All.   A deed without a name.
Macbeth. I conjure you, by that which you   50
   profess,—
Howe'er you come to know it,—answer me:
Though you untie the winds and let them fight
Against the churches; though the yesty waves   53
Confound and swallow navigation up;   54
Though bladed corn be lodg'd and trees blown   55
   down;
Though castles topple on their warders' heads;
Though palaces and pyramids do slope   57
Their heads to their foundations; though the treasure
Of Nature's germens tumble all together,   59
Even till destruction sicken; answer me   60
To what I ask you.
First Witch.   Speak.
Second Witch.   Demand.
Third Witch.   We'll answer.   61
First Witch. Say if thou'dst rather hear it from our   62
   mouths,
Or from our masters'?
Macbeth.   Call 'em: let me see 'em.
First Witch. Pour in sow's blood, that hath eaten
     Her nine farrow; grease that's sweaten   65
     From the murderer's gibbet throw
     Into the flame.
All.   Come, high or low;   67
     Thyself and office deftly show.   68
   Thunder. First Apparition *of an armed Head.*
Macbeth. Tell me, thou unknown power,—
First Witch.   He knows thy thought:
Hear his speech, but say thou nought.   70
First Apparition. Macbeth! Macbeth! Macbeth!
   beware Macduff;
Beware the Thane of Fife. Dismiss me. Enough.
                    [*Descends.*
Macbeth. Whate'er thou art, for thy good caution
   thanks;
Thou hast harp'd my fear aright. But one word   74
   more,—
First Witch. He will not be commanded: here's
   another,
More potent than the first.
   Thunder. Second Apparition, *a bloody Child.*
Second Apparition. Macbeth! Macbeth!
   Macbeth!—
Macbeth. Had I three ears, I'd hear thee.
Second Apparition. Be bloody, bold, and resolute;
   laugh to scorn
The power of man, for none of woman born
Shall harm Macbeth.   [*Descends.*
Macbeth. Then live, Macduff: what need I fear of
   thee?
But yet I'll make assurance double sure,
And take a bond of fate: thou shalt not live;   84
That I may tell pale hearted fear it lies,

46

---

50. "conjure": call upon solemnly, by oath.

53. "yesty": foaming.

54. "Confound": destroy, ruin.

55. "lodg'd": laid flat.

57. "slope": let fall.
   "pyramids": steeple (a common usage of the time).

59. "Nature's germens": the seeds of all life in nature.

60. "sicken": grow weary of destroying.

61. "Demand": ask.

62-3. "Say . . . masters' ": The Sisters give Macbeth his choice between visions and mere prophecy.

65. "nine farrow": litter of pigs.

67. "high or low": in the upper or lower air.

68. "office": function.
   "deftly": skillfully, smartly.

70. Notice how the witches's attitude towards Macbeth has changed since I,iii.

74. "harp'd . . . aright": expressed it truly.

84. "take . . . fate": bind fate, as securely as with a legal bond, to fulfil this prediction of safety (by killing Macduff himself).

MACBETH

ACT IV SCENE I

in the stage. The same device will have already accomplished the disappearance of the witches in I,iii, and of Banquo's ghost in III,iv.

The procession of kings would be costumed and performed with the most stately magnificence both for its spectacular effect (the utmost contrast with the grotesque witches and degraded Macbeth) and because it is a full dress tribute to James I and the Stuart dynasty. For the identity of the eight Stuart kings (Banquo's descendants) see the geneological table in the introduction. Mary, Queen of Scots is eliminated from the procession, probably on account of her sex and religion. At any rate the eighth king, holding the mirror to indicate his endless succession of rulers of both realms, would be James I.

The passage from line 126 to line 132 including the dance of the witches with Hecate (again because of its iambic verse and redundant spectacle) is assumed to be another addition by Middleton (see above, and III,v). If so (and it is likely), it is far more effective than the others. Eliminate Hecate, make the dance a hideous improvisation by the witches (with the simplest music, and very short), and the effect would be one of telling irony and mockery of "this great king."

The closing speech is fifth in the series in which Macbeth redefines the role he will play. The fact that he speaks his mind this time without caution in the presence of Lennox indicates the irrational security he has taken from the latest prophecies. He has seen his attempt to secure himself through crafty villainy fail as a result of both supernatural interference and the swift march of events. Now, believing what chimes in with his wishes, he takes assurance of a charmed life. He decides therefore to act on impulse, and outrace time. Can we understand why his impulse takes the form it does of raging tyranny and destruction? Having witnessed in our century the rise and fall of dictatorships, we are in a better position to understand than some of our forebears. Impulsive action is easier than thoughtful restraint and he has already toyed with the idea of such immediate self-expression several times, e.g., I,vii,1-2, II,i,60-1, III,iv,139-40.

And sleep in spite of thunder.
Thunder. Third Apparition, *a Child crowned, with a tree in his hand.*
What is this,
That rises like the issue of a king,   87
And wears upon his baby brow the round
And top of sovereignty?   89
All. Listen but speak not to 't.
Third Apparition. Be lion-mettled, proud, and take no care
Who chafes, who frets, or where conspirers are: 91
Macbeth shall never vanquish'd be until
Great Birnam Wood to high Dunsinane Hill
Shall come against him.   [*Descends.*
Macbeth. That will never be:
Who can impress the forest, bid the tree   95
Unfix his earth-bound root? Sweet bodements!   96
good!
Rebellion's head, rise never till the wood
Of Birnam rise, and our high-plac'd Macbeth
Shall live the lease of nature, pay his breath   99
To time and mortal custom. Yet my heart   100
Throbs to know one thing: tell me—if your art
Can tell so much,—shall Banquo's issue ever
Reign in this kingdom?
All. Seek to know no more.
Macbeth. I will be satisfied: deny me this,   104
And an eternal curse fall on you! Let me know.
Why sinks that cauldron? and what noise is this?   106
[*Hautboys.*
First Witch. Show!
Second Witch. Show!
Third Witch. Show!
All. Show his eyes, and grieve his heart;   111
Come like shadows, so depart.
A show of Eight Kings; the last with a glass in his hand:
BANQUO'S GHOST *following.*
Macbeth. Thou art too like the spirit of Banquo;   112
down!
Thy crown does sear mine eyeballs: and thy hair,
Thou other gold-bound brow, is like the first:
A third is like the former. Filthy hags!
Why do you show me this? A fourth! Start, eyes!
What! will the line stretch out to the crack of doom?
Another yet? A seventh! I'll see no more:
And yet the eighth appears, who bears a glass   119
Which shows me many more; and some I see
That two-fold balls and treble sceptres carry   121
Horrible sight! Now, I see, 'tis true;
For the blood-bolter'd Banquo smiles upon me,   123
And points at them for his. [*Apparitions vanish.*
What! is this so?
First Witch. Ay, sir, all this is so: but why
Stands Macbeth thus amazedly?
Come sisters, cheer we up his sprites,   127
And show the best of our delights.
I'll charm the air to give a sound,
While you perform your antick round,   130
That this great king may kindly say

Stage direction: "a Child crowned": refers to Malcolm who became king.

87. "like": in the shape of

89. "top": diadem.

91. "chafes": is resentful.

95. "impress": enlist forcibly.

96. "bodements": prophecies.

99. "lease": appointed time. The whole clause takes its metaphor from the laws of rental.

100. "mortal custom": dying, which is common to all men.

104. "I will be satisfied": I want full information.

106. "noise": music.

111. "Show": a dumb show, a pantomime.

112. "Thou . . . Banquo": said to the first of the Eight Kings.

119. "glass": mirror.

121. "balls": insignia of sovereignty.

123. "blood-bolter'd": having his hair matted with blood.

127. "sprites": spirits.

130. "round" dance in a circle.

47

MACBETH

This scene is often omitted from performances of the play because it adds nothing absolutely necessary to the story. It is relevant to the theme, however, in that it offers a picture of the brutal disorder of the country: division of families, anxiety, dismay, and slaughter. It is worthwhile for Ross's moving description of life in a police state (ll. 18-25) if it had nothing else in it.

For Ross's weeping see I,iv,35 and commentary.

Our duties did his welcome pay.   132
        [*Music. The Witches dance, and then*
                    vanish with HECATE.
Macbeth. Where are they? Gone? Let this
   pernicious hour
Stand aye accursed in the calendar!
Come in, without there!

           Enter LENNOX.
Lennox.   What's your Grace's will?   135
Macbeth. Saw you the weird sisters?
Lennox.   No, my lord.
Macbeth. Came they not by you?
Lennox.   No indeed, my lord.
Macbeth. Infected be the air whereon they ride,
And damn'd all those that trust them! I did hear   139
The galloping of horse: who was 't came by?
Lennox. 'Tis two or three, my lord, that bring you
   word
Macduff is fled to England.
Macbeth.   Fled to England!
Lennox. Ay, my good lord.
Macbeth. Time, thou anticipat'st my dread
   exploits;   144
The flighty purpose never is o'ertook
Unless the deed go with it; from this moment
The very firstlings of my heart shall be   147
The firstlings of my hand. And even now,
To crown my thoughts with acts, be it thought and
   done;
The castle of Macduff I will surprise;
Seize upon Fife; give to the edge of the sword
His wife, his babes, and all unfortunate souls   152
That trace him in his line. No boasting like a
   fool;   153
This deed I'll do before this purpose cool:
But no more sights! Where are these gentlemen?   155
Come, bring me where they are.   [*Exeunt.*

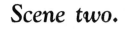

Scene two.

(FIFE. MACDUFF'S CASTLE)

Enter LADY MACDUFF, *her Son, and* ROSS.

Lady Macduff. What had he done to make him fly
   the land?
Ross. You must have patience, madam.
Lady Macduff.   He had none:
His flight was madness: when our actions do not,   3
Our fears do make us traitors.
Ross.   You know not
Whether it was his wisdom or his fear.
Lady Macduff. Wisdom! to leave his wife, to leave
   his babes,
His mansion and his titles in a place   7
From whence himself does fly? He loves us not;
He wants the natural touch; for the poor wren,   9

132. Macbeth has not welcomed the Sisters. Their meaning is teasing and ironical.

Stage direction: "with Hecate": Hecate will have been standing at the back of the stage throughout (see I.44, and commentary).

135. Lennox is one of Macbeth's most trusted advisors, but we know that he is ringleader of a conspiracy against him.

139. "damn'd": Macbeth unknowingly curses himself.

144. "anticipat'st": forestall, prevent

147. "firstlings": first born.

152. "unfortunate": a remnant of "human kindness" (See I, v, 18).

153. "trace": follow.

155. "these gentlemen": these who brought the news.

3-4. "when . . . traitors": Macduff had done nothing treasonable, yet fear had made him flee to the English court, making him a traitor.

7. "his titles": all his hereditary possessions.

9. "the . . . touch": the instinct which prompts all creatures to defend their young.

MACBETH

ACT IV SCENE II

The dialogue between Lady Macduff and her son shows in the saucy wisdom of the child the overriding cynicism of the time. There is a striking similarity between lines 54-6, and a passage in BASILIKON DORON. If a king is too lenient, said King James, "the offences would soon come to such heaps and the contempt of you grow so great, that when ye would fall to punish, the number of them to be punished would exceed the innocent." There was great severity being exercised in England, following the Gunpowder Plot (1605), against treason, especially that of Catholics who were forced by circumstances, if they were devout, to swear and lie.

The most diminutive of birds, will fight—
Her young ones in her nest—against the owl. 11
All is the fear and nothing is the love;
As little is the wisdom, where the flight
So runs against all reason.
   Ross.   My dearest coz,
I pray you, school yourself: but, for your husband, 15
He is noble, wise, judicious, and best knows
The fits o' the season. I dare not speak much further: 17
But cruel are the times, when we are traitors
And do not know ourselves, when we hold rumour 19
From what we fear, yet know not what we fear,
But float upon a wild and violent sea
Each way and move. I take my leave of you:
Shall not be long but I'll be here again.
Things at the worst will cease, or else climb upward 24
To what they were before. My pretty cousin, 25
Blessing upon you!
   Lady Macduff. Father'd he is, and yet he's fatherless.
   Ross. I am so much a fool, should I stay longer,
It would be my disgrace, and your discomfort: 29
I take my leave at once.   [*Exit.*
   Lady Macduff.   Sirrah, your father's dead: 30
And what will you do now? How will you live?
   Son. As birds do, mother.
   Lady Macduff.   What! with worms and flies?
   Son. With what I get, I mean; and so do they.
   Lady Macduff. Poor bird! thou'dst never fear the
      net nor lime, 34
The pit-fall nor the gin. 35
   Son. Why should I, mother? Poor birds they are 36
      not set for.
My father is not dead, for all your saying.
   Lady Macduff. Yes, he is dead: how wilt thou do
      for a father?
   Son. Nay, how will you do for a husband?
   Lady Macduff. Why, I can buy me twenty at any
      market.
   Son. Then you'll buy 'em to sell again.
   Lady Macduff. Thou speak'st with all thy wit; and
      yet, i' faith, 42
With wit enough for thee.
   Son. Was my father a traitor, mother?
   Lady Macduff. Ay, that he was.
   Son. What is a traitor?
   Lady Macduff. Why, one that swears and lies. 47
   Son. And be all traitors that do so?
   Lady Macduff. Every one that does so is a traitor,
      and must be hanged.
   Son. And must they all be hanged that swear and
      lie?
   Lady Macduff. Every one.
   Son. Who must hang them?
   Lady Macduff. Why, the honest men.
   Son. Then the liars and swearers are fools, for there
are liars and swearers enow to beat the honest men,
and hang up them.
   Lady Macduff. Now God help thee, poor monkey!
But how wilt thou do for a father?
   Son. If he were dead, you'd weep for him: if you

11. "in her nest": therefore in her charge.

15. "school yourself": control yourself. "for": as for.

17. "The fits o' the season": the irregular happenings of the time.

19. "do not know ourselves": know ourselves to be traitors.

   "hold rumour," etc.: We are ready to believe rumors which are in accord with our fears.

24. "climb upward": take a turn for the better.

25. "My pretty cousin": Ross turns to speak to the boy.

29. "my disgrace": to disgrace himself by weeping.

30. "Sirrah": often(to boys) as a playful and affectionate term.

34. "lime": a sticky substance for trapping birds.

35. "pit-fall": a kind of trap. "gin": short for engine, used for any contrivance.

36. "they": the net, trap, etc.

42-3. "Thou . . . thee": What you say shows but a child's wisdom, yet for a child, your wit is pretty good.

47. "one . . . lies": one who takes an oath and breaks it. The term was commonly used also for people who, through perjury or equivocation, swore oaths against their convictions. Thus a topical reference to the gunpowder plot may be assumed.

MACBETH

ACT IV SCENE II

Cf. "Fair is foul, and foul is fair." (I,i,11.)

ACT IV SCENE III

This is the longest and one of the most static scenes in the play. Its action is all in the minds of the characters preparing the future and digesting the past. It is the only scene in the play not set in Scotland, thus we may look for details to point up the symbolic contrast between orderly England and disordered Scotland, the light and the dark (see also III,vi, and commentary). The scene may be divided into three sections: first, the overcoming of division between Malcolm and Macduff; second, the representation of gracious England; third, the news from Scotland.

The interview between Malcolm and Macduff is the weakest thing in the play because Malcolm's device to test Macduff's honor is unnatural and unconvincing.

would not, it were a good sign that I should quickly
have a new father.
Lady Macduff. Poor prattler, how thou talk'st!

Enter a Messenger.

Messenger. Bless you, fair dame! I am not to you
known,
Though in your state of honour I am perfect. 64
I doubt some danger does approach you nearly: 65
If you will take a homely man's advice, 66
Be not found here; hence, with your little ones.
To fright you thus, methinks, I am too savage;
To do worse to you were fell cruelty, 69
Which is too nigh your person. Heaven preserve
you!
I dare abide no longer. [*Exit.*
Lady Macduff. Whither should I fly? 71
I have done no harm. But I remember now
I am in this earthly world, where to do harm
Is often laudable, to do good sometime 74
Accounted dangerous folly; why then, alas!
Do I put up that womanly defence,
To say I have done no harm?

Enter Murderers.

What are these faces?
Murderer. Where is your husband?
Lady Macduff. I hope in no place so unsanctified
Where such as thou mayst find him.
Murderer. He's a traitor.
Son. Thou liest, thou shag-ear'd villain.
Murderer. What, you egg! 81
Young fry of treachery! [*Stabbing him.*
Son. He has killed me, mother: 82
Run away, I pray you! [*Dies.*
[*Exit* LADY MACDUFF, *crying 'Murder',
and pursued by the* Murderers.

Scene three.

(ENGLAND. BEFORE THE KING'S PALACE)

Enter MALCOLM *and* MACDUFF.

Malcolm. Let us seek out some desolate shade, and
there
Weep our sad bosoms empty.
Macduff. Let us rather
Hold fast the mortal sword, and like good men 3
Bestride our down-fall'n birthdom; each new morn 4
New widows howl, new orphans cry, new sorrows
Strike heaven on the face, that it resounds 6
As if it felt with Scotland and yell'd out
Like syllable of dolour.
Malcolm. What I believe I'll wail, 8
What know believe; and what I can redress,
As I shall find the time to friend, I will. 10
What you have spoke, it may be so perchance.
This tyrant, whose sole name blisters our tongues, 12

64. "in your . . . perfect": I'm aware of your rank.

65. "doubt": fear.

66. "homely": of no high rank.

69. "fell": fierce.

71. "I dare," etc.: It would be death to myself to be discovered giving you information.

74. "sometime": sometimes.

81. "shag-ear'd": The long shaggy hair falling over the ruffian's ears reminds the boy of a dog's ears.

82. "fry": spawn.

Macduff has described to Malcolm the oppressive rule of Macbeth, and has offered his services if Malcolm will take command. But Malcolm suspects trickery to get him into Macbeth's power.

3. "mortal": deadly.

4. "Bestride": stand over to defend.

6. "that": so that.

8. "Like syllable of dolour": similar sounds of grief.

10. "As . . . friend": when the time seems ripe.

12. "sole": mere.

MACBETH

ACT IV SCENE III

Shakespeare took it directly out of Holinshed's CHRONICLE with only slight changes, and it drags badly, putting a great strain on the actors to make it pass. Down to line 45 all is well; it is both natural and dramatic that Malcolm should be suspicious of anyone coming from Scotland.

Hollowness sets in when Malcolm poses as a villian. It is out of character for a deceitful villian to describe himself with such disapproval in an effort to destroy his own opportunity. It is stupid for Macduff, who so acutely judged Macbeth in II,iii, to be impressed with Malcolm's self-slander. Further it is not even clear why Macduff's professed anguish should banish Malcolm's suspicions, though a first-rate actor could make it plausible.

Only the desire to follow historical facts and to present, by defining its opposite, a picture of a good king can excuse Shakespeare's use of this material.

Many of King James's political ideas are echoed. In lines 19-20, the doctrine is exemplified that a subject's duty is to obey his crowned king, that the guilt for a criminal action carried out by a subject against his own conscience is entirely the king's, and that if the subject follows conscience instead of command, he is guilty of treason (cf. references to Macduff as a traitor in IV,ii. It is a sign of disorder when conscience conflicts with duty). King James had put it thus: (BASILIKON DORON) "A tyrant's miserable and infamous life armeth in the end his own subjects . . . although that rebellion be ever unlawful on their part."

For some time now we have felt two currents of sympathy in the play, one for Macbeth's victims, the other for Macbeth himself. The first leads us to welcome the action of the forces of order aiming at the tyrant's destruction. The second, the tragic emotion, is simply on our hands; it has not the support of our moral judgment, but we see Macbeth's bitter anguish and understand how it came about. To understand is to sympathize, especially when the blame is divided. Macbeth's goodness is not dead; it has become the irritant that drives his malice.

Here is Holinshed's version of this dialogue: (Malcolm) "First such immoderate lust and voluptuous sensuality (the abominable fountain of all vices) followeth me that if I were made King of Scots, I should seek to deflower your maids and matrons in such wise

Was once thought honest; you have lov'd him well; 13
He hath not touch'd you yet. I am young; but something 14
You may deserve of him through me, and wisdom 15
To offer up a weak, poor, innocent lamb
To appease an angry god.
Macduff. I am not treacherous.
Malcolm. But Macbeth is.
A good and virtuous nature may recoil 19
In an imperial charge. But I shall crave your pardon;
That which you are my thoughts cannot transpose; 21
Angels are bright still, though the brightest fell; 22
Though all things foul would wear the brows of grace, 23
Yet grace must still look so.
Macduff. I have lost my hopes. 24
Malcolm. Perchance even there where I did find my doubts. 25
Why in that rawness left you wife and child— 26
Those precious motives, those strong knots of love— 27
Without leave-taking? I pray you,
Let not my jealousies be your dishonours, 29
But mine own safeties: you may be rightly just, 30
Whatever I shall think.
Macduff. Bleed, bleed, poor country!
Great tyranny, lay thou thy basis sure, 32
For goodness dare not check thee! wear thou thy wrongs; 33
The title is affeer'd! Fare thee well, lord: 34
I would not be the villain that thou think'st
For the whole space that's in the tyrant's grasp,
And the rich East to boot.
Malcolm. Be not offended:
I speak not as in absolute fear of you.
I think our country sinks beneath the yoke;
It weeps, it bleeds, and each new day a gash
Is added to her wounds: I think withal 41
There would be hands uplifted in my right;
And here from gracious England have I offer 43
Of goodly thousands: but, for all this, 44
When I shall tread upon the tyrant's head,
Or wear it on my sword, yet my poor country 46
Shall have more vices than it had before,
More suffer, and more sundry ways than ever,
By him that shall succeed.
Macduff. What should he be? 49
Malcolm. It is myself I mean; in whom I know
All the particulars of vice so grafted, 51
That, when they shall be open'd, black Macbeth 52
Will seem as pure as snow, and the poor state
Esteem him as a lamb, being compar'd
With my confineless harms.
Macduff. Not in the legions 55
Of horrid hell can come a devil more damn'd
In evils to top Macbeth.
Malcolm. I grant him bloody, 57
Luxurious, avaricious, false, deceitful, 58
Sudden, malicious, smacking of every sin 59
That has a name; but there's no bottom, none,
In my voluptuousness: your wives, your daughters,

13. "honest": good, honorable, noble.

14. "I am young; but . . .": Though I am young, I can see that . . . .

15. "deserve": win, earn.
"through me": by betraying me to Macbeth.
"and wisdom": and it is wisdom.

19-20. "recoil . . . charge": give way under pressure from a monarch.

21. "tranpose": transform. My suspicion cannot alter the fact of your honor, if you are as you say.

22. "the brightest": Lucifer.

23. "the brows of grace": seeming goodness.

24. "so": like herself, like virtue.

25. This line makes sense if Macduff's hope was to put Malcolm in Macbeth's power (as Malcolm assumes).

26. "rawness": raw haste.

27. "motives": incentives to action.

29. "jealousies": suspicious cares.

30. "rightly just": perfectly honorable and good.

32. "basis": foundation.

33. "check thee": call thee to account.

34. "affeer'd": legally confirmed. Macbeth's title is established beyond dispute, since Malcolm refuses to contest it.

41. "withal": also, besides.

43. "England": the king of England.

44. "but . . . this": At this point Malcolm's device for testing Macduff begins.

46. "yet": after all that, emphatic.

49. "What . . . be": What worse king could there be than Macbeth?

51. "particulars": particular kinds, special varieties.

52. "open'd": The figure is from the opening of a bud, suggested by "grafted."

55. "confineless harms": the boundless injuries that I should do to my people.

57. "top": surpass.

58. "Luxurious": lascivious.

59. "Sudden": violent.

MACBETH

ACT IV SCENE III

that mine intemperance should be more importable unto you than the bloody tyranny of Macbeth now is."

(Macbeth) "This surely is a very evil fault, for many noble princes and kings have lost both lives and kingdoms for the same; nevertheless there are women enough in Scotland. . . ."

(Malcolm) "I am also the most avaricious creature on the earth, so that if I were king, I should seek so many ways to get the lands and goods that I would slay the most part of all the nobles of Scotland by surmised accusations, to the end I might enjoy their lands, goods, and possessions. . . ."

(Macduff) "(This is a far worse fault) for avarice is the root of all mischief, and for that crime the most part of our kings have been slain and brought to their final end. . . . There's gold enough in Scotland to satisfy thy greedy desire."

(Malcolm) "I am furthermore inclined to dissimulation. . . . Then, sith there is nothing so becometh a prince than constancy, verity, truth, and justice . . . you see how unable I am to Govern any region or province. . . ."

(Macduff) "Oh, ye unhappy and miserable Scottishmen. . . . A cursed and wicked tyrant that now reigneth over you, without any right or title. . . . This other, that hath the right to the crown, is so replete with the inconstant behaviour and manifest vices of Englishman [cf. "English epicures." V,iii,8. Shakespeare puts this traditional Scottish opinion into Macbeth's mouth, as an error, because his symbolic pattern requires a virtuous England.] . . . . Adieu, Scotland, for I now account myself a banished man."

"God above deal . . .", comes like a benediction, as unity and concord replaces the division between them.

Your matrons, and your maids, could not fill up
The cistern of my lust, and my desire   63
All continent impediments would o'erbear   64
That did oppose my will; better Macbeth   65
That such an one to reign.

Macduff.   Boundless intemperance   66
In nature is a tyranny; it hath been
Th' untimely emptying of the happy throne,
And fall of many kings. But fear not yet   69
To take upon you what is yours; you may
Convey your pleasures in a spacious plenty,   71
And yet seem cold, the time you may so hoodwink. 72
We have willing dames enough; there cannot be
That vulture in you, to devour so many
As will to greatness dedicate themselves,   75
Finding it so inclin'd.

Malcolm.   With this there grows   76
In my most ill-compos'd affection such   77
A stanchless avarice that, were I king,   78
I should cut off the nobles for their lands,
Desire his jewels and his other's house;   80
And my more-having would be as a sauce   81
To make me hunger more, that I should forge   82
Quarrels unjust against the good and loyal,   83
Destroying them for wealth.

Macduff.   This avarice
Sticks deeper, grows with more pernicious root 85
Than summer-seeming lust, and it hath been   86
The sword of our slain kings: yet do not fear;
Scotland hath foisons to fill up your will,   88
Of your mere own; all these are portable,   89
With other graces weigh'd.

Malcolm. But I have none: the king-becoming
          graces,
As justice, verity, temperance, stableness,
Bounty, perseverance, mercy, lowliness,
Devotion, patience, courage, fortitude,
I have no relish of them, but abound   95
In the division of each several crime,
Acting it many ways. Nay, had I power, I should
Pour the sweet milk of concord into hell,
Uproar the universal peace, confound   99
All unity on earth.

Macduff.   O Scotland, Scotland!

Malcolm. If such a one be fit to govern, speak:
I am as I have spoken.

Macduff.   Fit to govern!
No, not to live. O nation miserable,
With an untitled tyrant bloody-scepter'd,   104
When shalt thou see thy wholesome days again,
Since that the truest issue of thy throne
By his own interdiction stands accurs'd,   107
And does blaspheme his breed? Thy royal father
Was a most sainted king; the queen that bore thee,
Oft'ner upon her knees than on her feet,
Died every day she liv'd. Fare thee well!   111
These evils thou repeat'st upon thyself
Have banish'd me from Scotland. O my breast,
Thy hope ends here!

Malcolm.   Macduff, this noble passion, 114

63. "cistern": tank, vat.

64. "continent impediments": restraining limits.

65. "will": desire.

66-7. "Boundless . . . tyranny": Boundless intemperance usurps absolute sway over all his other qualities.

69. "yet": in spite of all you have said.

71. "Convey": manage craftily or secretly.

72. "time": the times, the people.

75. "dedicate": offer up.

76. "Finding": if they find.

77. "ill-compos'd affection": character made up of evil elements.

78. "stanchless": insatiable.

80. "his": this man's.

81. "more-having": increase in wealth.

82. "forge": devise falsely.

83. "Quarrels": charges.

85. "Sticks deeper": is less easily uprooted.

86. "summer-seeming": befitting only the summertime of life, and therefore not lasting as long as avarice.

88. "foisons": abundant supplies.

89. "portable": bearable.

95. "relish": trace, taste.

95-6. "abound . . . crime": I am guilty of every possible form of each sin.

99. "Uproar": change to tumultuous strife.

104. "tyrant": usurper.

107. "interdiction": under the ban of the Church; a curse excluding one from the throne.

111. "Died . . . liv'd": referring to penances and religious exercises by which she renounces the world.

114. "passion": strong emotion.

MACBETH

ACT IV SCENE III

The contrast between Edward and Macbeth, already suggested in III,vi, is here sharply focused. Macbeth murders; Edward heals. Macbeth is damned; Edward is sanctified. Heaven prophesies in England through the king; hell prophesies in Scotland to the king. It is curious to recall in this connection that Edward the Confessor, besides his famous piety, symbolized purity to the popular imagination through his white hair and transparent complexion. (He was in fact likely an albino.)

Touching to cure the King's Evil (Scrofula) was begun by Edward the Confessor, and continued by the English rulers down to 1719, when Queen Anne touched Samuel Johnson, the famous man of letters, then a child. Now the superstitious sort believed in this power, and even regarded its successful employment as proof of a monarch's right to the throne. Queen Elizabeth had made much of it as a means of gaining the gratitude of her people. Part of the ceremony was the presentation of the angel, a gold coin especially minted for this ceremony, which was hung by the sovereign as a medallion around the patient's neck. King James had at first refused to perform this ceremony, which he considered superstitious, and not until 1605 did he reinstate the full ceremony. (The first angels minted in his reign are dated 1605.)

The passage, besides its symbolic function in the drama, had double significance as a topical recognition of King James's gracious compliance with the desires of his subjects.

Ross's description of Scotland's plight, echoing Macduff's (ll. 4-8) serves to point the symbolic contrast with England.

Child of integrity, hath from my soul 115
Wip'd the black scruples, reconcil'd my thoughts
To thy good truth and honour. Devilish Macbeth
By many of these trains hath sought to win me 118
Into his power, and modest wisdom plucks me 119
From over-credulous haste; but God above
Deal between thee and me! for even now 121
I put myself to thy direction, and 122
Unspeak mine own detraction, here abjure 123
The taints and blames I laid upon myself,
For strangers to my nature. I am yet 125
Unknown to woman, never was forsworn, 126
Scarcely have coveted what was mine own;
At no time broke my faith, would not betray
The devil to his fellow, and delight
No less in truth than life; my first false speaking
Was this upon myself. What I am truly, 131
Is thine and my poor country's to command;
Whither indeed, before thy here-approach,
Old Siward, with ten thousand war-like men,
Already at a point, was setting forth. 135
Now we'll together, and the chance of goodness 136
Be like our warranted quarrel. Why are you silent?
Macduff. Such welcome and unwelcome things at once
    'Tis hard to reconcile.

Enter a Doctor.

Malcolm. Well; more anon. Comes the king forth, I pray you?
Doctor. Ay, sir; there are a crew of wretched souls
That stay his cure; their malady convinces 142
The great assay of art; but, at his touch, 143
Such sanctity hath heaven given his hand,
They presently amend.
    Malcolm.   I thank you, doctor.
            [*Exit* Doctor.
Macduff. What's the disease he means?
Malcolm.   'Tis called the evil: 146
A most miraculous work in this good king,
Which often, since my here-remain in England, 148
I have seen him do. How he solicits heaven,
Himself best knows; but strangely-visited people, 150
All swoln and ulcerous, pitiful to the eye,
The mere despair of surgery, he cures, 152
Hanging a golden stamp about their necks, 153
Put on with holy prayers; and 'tis spoken,
To the succeeding royalty he leaves
The healing benediction. With this strange virtue, 156
He hath a heavenly gift of prophecy,
And sundry blessings hang about his throne
That speak him full of grace.

Enter ROSS.

Macduff.   See, who comes here? 159
Malcolm. My countryman; but yet I know him not.
Macduff. My ever-gentle cousin, welcome hither.
Malcolm. I know him now. Good God, betimes 162
    remove
The means that makes us strangers! 163
Ross.   Sir, amen.

115. "Child of integrity": which can proceed only from integrity of character.

118. "trains": plots.

119. "modest wisdom": wise moderation, prudent caution.
    "plucks me": restrains me.

121. "Deal . . . me": Be judge between us in the matter.

122. "to thy direction": under thy guidance.

123. "abjure": deny solemnly, as upon oath.

125. "For . . . nature": as being quite foreign to my actual character.

126. "forsworn": an oath-breaker.

131. "upon": against.

135. "at a point": fully prepared.

136-7. "the chance . . . quarrel": May our chance of success be as good as our cause is just.

142. "stay": await.
    "convinces": baffles.

143. "The . . . art": the utmost efforts of medical science.

146. "the evil": scrofula or the king's evil, so called because it was thought to be cured by the royal touch.

148. "my here-remain": my sojourn here.

150. "strangely-visited": afflicted with hideous disease.

152. "mere": utter.

153. "stamp": a coin which the king gave to the patient whom he touched.

156. "virtue": healing power.

159. "grace": sanctity, holiness.

162. "betimes": speedily.

163. "The means": i.e., Macbeth.

MACBETH

ACT IV SCENE III

Ross's reluctance to report Macduff's bereavement produces telling irony, and recalls Macbeth's, "Duncan is in his grave;/ After life's fitful fever he sleeps well," etc. (III,ii,22-6), and Lady Macbeth's, "'Tis safer to be that which we destroy . . ." (III,ii,6-7). All these speeches equating death (sleep's counterfeit) with peace help to prepare the rise of the wish for death soon to overtake Lady Macbeth and her husband.

The word Christendom here, together with the frequent references to God throughout the scene, serves to enlarge the forthcoming action to the supernatural plane: sacred order and right versus infernal disorder and wrong.

Macduff. Stands Scotland where it did?
Ross.   Alas! poor country;
Almost afraid to know itself. It cannot   165
Be call'd our mother, but our grave; where nothing,
But who knows nothing, is once seen to smile;   167
Where sighs and groans and shrieks that rent the air   168
Are made, not mark'd; where violent sorrow seems   169
A modern ecstacy; the dead man's knell   170
Is there scarce ask'd for who; and good men's lives
Expire before the flowers in their caps,   172
Dying or ere they sicken.
Macduff.   O! relation   173
Too nice, and yet too true!
Malcolm.   What's the newest brief?   174
Ross. That of an hour's age doth hiss the speaker;   175
Each minute teems a new one.
Macduff.   How does my wife?
Ross. Why, well.
Macduff.   And all my children?
Ross.   Well too.   177
Macduff. The tyrant has not batter'd at their
        peace?
Ross. No; they were well at peace when I did
        leave 'em.
Macduff. Be not a niggard of your speech: how
        goes 't?
Ross. When I came hither to transport the tidings,
Which I have heavily borne, there ran a rumour   182
Of many worthy fellows that were out;   183
Which was to my belief witness'd the rather
For that I saw the tyrant's power a-foot.   185
Now is the time of help; your eye in Scotland
Would create soldiers, make our women fight,
To doff their dire distresses.
Malcolm.   Be 't their comfort
We are coming thither. Gracious England hath   189
Lent us good Siward and ten thousand men;
An older and a better soldier none   191
That Christendom gives out.
Ross.   Would I could answer   192
This comfort with the like! But I have words
That would be howl'd out in the desert air,   194
Where hearing should not latch them.
Macduff.   What concern they?   195
The general cause? or is it a fee-grief   196
Due to some single breast?
Ross.   No mind that's honest   197
But in it shares some woe, though the main part
Pertains to you alone.
Macduff.   If it be mine
Keep it not from me; quickly let me have it.
Ross. Let not your ears despise my tongue for ever,
Which shall possess them with the heaviest sound   202
That ever yet they heard.
Macduff.   Hum! I guess at it.
Ross. Your castle is surpris'd; your wife and   204
        babes
Savagely slaughter'd; to relate the manner,
Were, on the quarry of these murder'd deer,   206
To add the death of you.

165. "to know itself": to look its own misfortunes in the face.

167. "who": one who.

168. "rent": rip or tear apart.

169. "not mark'd": because they are so common.

170. "A modern ecstacy": a fad.

172. "flowers": It was an Elizabethan fashion to wear a flower in the cap.

173. "or ere": before, i.e., by violence.

174. "Too nice": too minutely accurate.

175. "That . . . speaker": Telling an hour ago's dreadful news would get the teller a hissing for bringing stale news.

177. "well": intentionally ambiguous; often used in breaking bad news gently. It means not only in good health, but also well off, i.e., in heaven.

182. "heavily": sadly.

183. "out": in the field, under arms.

185. "For that": because.
    "power": forces, troops.
    "a-foot": in motion, mobilized.

189. "England": the King of England.

191. "none": there is none.

192. "gives out": proclaims.

194. "would be": require to be, should be.

195. "latch": catch.

196. "a fee-grief": one that belongs to him alone.

197. "honest": good and honorable.

202. "heaviest": saddest.

204. "surpris'd": seized, captured.

206. "quarry": slaughtered bodies.

MACBETH

ACT IV SCENE III

The reticent grief of Macduff before his vow of vengeance, and the awkward and inexperienced, though well-meant, efforts of young Malcolm to help him through the crisis, provide an instance of Shakespeare's precious talent for the human touch.

The last line is significant. It recalls to our ears a moment from the beginning of the tragedy when Macbeth in his first tussle with temptation says, "Time and the hour run through the roughest day" (I,iii,147). Such reminders of the old Macbeth deepen our tragic sympathy. The balanced opposition of the two lines is neat. In the first, time moves day unavoidably towards night, both actual and symbolic (see II,iv,6-7); in the second it moves night towards day. The direction of the action, like a pendulum, has altered since the banquet.

Malcolm.　　　　Merciful heaven!
What! man; ne'er pull your hat upon your brows; 208
Give sorrow words; the grief that does not speak
Whispers the o'er-fraught heart and bids it break. 210
　Macduff. My children too?
Ross.　　　　Wife, children, servants, all
That could be found.
　Macduff.　　　And I must be from thence! 212
My wife kill'd too?
Ross.　　　I have said.
　Malcolm.　　　　Be comforted:
Let's make us medicine of our great revenge,
To cure this deadly grief.
　Macduff. He has no children. All my pretty ones?
Did you say all? O hell-kite! All? 217
What! all my pretty chickens and their dam
At one fell swoop?
　Malcolm.　　　Dispute it like a man.
　Macduff.　　　　I shall do so; 219
But I must also feel it as a man:
I cannot but remember such things were,
That were most precious to me. Did heaven look on,
And would not take their part? Sinful Macduff!
They were all struck for thee. Naught that I am, 224
Not for their own demerits, but for mine,
Fell slaughter on their souls. Heaven rest them
　　now!
　Malcolm. Be this the whetstone of your sword:
　　let grief
Convert to anger; blunt not the heart, enrage it.
　Macduff. O! I could play the woman with mine 229
　　eyes,
And braggart with my tongue. But, gentle heavens, 230
Cut short all intermission; front to front 231
Bring thou this fiend of Scotland and myself;
Within my sword's length set him; if he 'scape,
Heaven forgive him too!
　Malcolm.　　　　This tune goes manly. 234
Come, go we to the king; our power is ready;
Our lack is nothing but our leave. Macbeth 236
Is ripe for shaking, and the powers above
Put on their instruments. Receive what cheer you
　　may; 238
The night is long that never finds the day. [*Exeunt.*

208. "pull . . . brows": become melancholy and brooding.

210. "Whispers . . . heart": whispers to the overburdened heart.

212. "And . . . thence": spoken in bitter self-reproach.

217. "hell-kite": hellish bird of prey.

219. "Dispute it": resist it, withstand your grief.

224. "Naught": worthless man.

229. "play . . . eyes": weep.

230. "braggart . . . tongue": rant.

231. "intermission": the time between now and our meeting.

234. "goes manly": has a manly sound.

236. "Our lack . . . leave": We wait only to take leave of those who will remain here.

238. "Put on their instruments": encourage, or urge forward their weapons, (tools or agents).

MACBETH

ACT V SCENE 1

The sleepwalking scene owes nothing to any source beyond Shakespeare's insight and dramatic sense. There is little in Lady Macbeth's previous action to prepare us for this pathos. It forces us to reinterpret her character. In her lonely idleness (see III,ii) she has had no occupation for her practical intelligence or her compulsive will, except to repress the paintings (see II,ii,54-6) of her imagination. But she cannot suppress them in sleep (cf. Banquo II,i,7-9) and the tender and passionate side of her nature (see I,vii,54-5, and II,ii,14-5) rises against her peace. What's done is not done with.

Dramatically, this quiet and touching episode, prevents the last act from degenerating into mere blood and thunder. Macbeth's capacity for complex suffering is just about burnt out. His madness has the effect of removing the richness of his personality, making him less than human unless we make an effort to recall his past. Such efforts are not made while an action is being watched. To prevent the loss of tragic feeling Shakespeare devised the formal pattern this scene reveals. While Macbeth passes from complex inward struggle through villainy into madness, Lady Macbeth follows an opposite course from hysterical obsession through villainy to complex inward disharmony. Thus the tragic sympathy for a richly suffering human being is distributed throughout the action, which otherwise, owing to Macbeth's necessarily early and decisive fall, would have dwindled.

The prose form is in keeping with the disordered ryhthm of sleep.

The scene is composed largely of confused memories, reviewing for us the tragic action of Act One, and of symbols reawakening the themes and oppositions which give enlarged meaning to the story. For example, the candle crystalizes the light/darkness symbolism. She has desired darkness ("Come thick night") and finds it horrible. Her candle is a pathetic attempt to dispel real darkness with artificial light. Among the references to the washing of her hands, "all the perfumes of Arabia . . ." balances and recalls Macbeth's "all great Neptune's ocean" (II,ii,60-3), and makes ironic contrast with, "A little water clears us of this deed:/ How easy it is then!" (II,ii,68-9). And how touching her characteristic line, "What's done is done" III,ii,12) sounds in this context (l.65).

ACT FIVE, scene one.

(DUNSINANE. A ROOM IN THE CASTLE)

Enter a Doctor of Physic *and a* Waiting-Gentlewoman.

Doctor. I have two nights watched with you, but can perceive no truth in your report. When was it she last walked?

Gentlewoman. Since his majesty went into the field, 5
I have seen her rise from her bed, throw her nightgown upon her, unlock her closet, take forth paper, fold it, write upon 't, read it, afterwards seal it, and again return to bed; yet all this while in a most fast sleep.

Doctor. A great perturbation in nature, to receive at once the benefit of sleep and do the effects of watching! In this slumbery agitation, besides her walking 13 and other actual performances, what, at any time, have you heard her say?

Gentlewoman. That, sir, which I will not report after her.

Doctor. You may to me, and 'tis most meet you 18 should.

Gentlewoman. Neither to you nor any one, having no witness to confirm my speech. 21

Enter LADY MACBETH, *with a taper.*

Lo you! here she comes. This is her very guise; and, 22
upon my life, fast asleep. Observe her; stand close. 23
Doctor. How came she by that light?
Gentlewoman. Why, it stood by her: she has light by her continually; 'tis her command.
Doctor. You see, her eyes are open.
Gentlewoman. Ay, but their sense is shut.
Doctor. What is it she does now? Look, how she rubs her hands.
Gentlewoman. It is an accustomed action with her, to seem thus washing her hands. I have known her to continue in this a quarter of an hour.
Lady Macbeth. Yet here's a spot. 34
Doctor. Hark! she speaks. I will set down what 35
comes from her, to satisfy my remembrance the more strongly.
Lady Macbeth. Out, damned spot! out, I say! One; 38
two: why, then 'tis time to do 't. Hell is murky! Fie, 39
my lord, fie! a soldier, and afeard? What need we fear who knows it, when none can call our power to account? Yet who would have thought the old man to have had so much blood in him?
Doctor. Do you mark that? 44
Lady Macbeth. The Thane of Fife had a wife: where 45
is she now? What! will these hands ne'er be clean? No more o' that, my lord, no more o' that: you mar all 47
with this starting.
Doctor. Go to, go to; you have known what you 49
should not.
Gentlewoman. She has spoke what she should not, I am sure of that: Heaven knows what she has known.

Stage direction: "a Waiting-Gentlewoman": a lady of the nobility, companion to the queen (not a mere servant).

5. "went into the field": took arms (see IV,iii,185).

13. "slumbery agitation": sleepy activity. The doctor's speech is rather wordy, part perhaps of his professional manner.

18. "meet": suitable.

21. "no witness": These are dangerous times, and the gentlewoman's words might, in the hands of an informer, bring a charge of treason against her.

22. "guise": manner.

23. "stand close": keep out of sight, hide.

34. "spot": i.e., of blood on her hand.

35. "set down": i.e., in a note book.

38-9. "One; two . . . do 't": a reference to the hour of Duncan's murder, or perhaps the ringing of the signal bell (II,i).

44. "mark": notice. This is an exclamation as much as it is a question.

45. "Thane of Fife": Macduff.

47. "my lord": Macbeth.

"mar all": spoil everything.

49. "go to": an exclamation indicating shocked amazement.

MACBETH

ACT V SCENE I

The divine is exactly what she cut herself off from.

"God, God forgive us all!" is a sudden expression of a typical tragic judgment meant to ring in the ears of the audience.

Macbeth's doctor balances that of King Eward (IV,iii). They provide a new symbolism for order and disorder (health and sickness) dramatically appropriate to the last stage of the plot (see also V,ii,27-9; V,iii).

ACT V SCENE II

Here we see Macbeth left further alone through the disintegration of his realm and household. The ominous name of Birnam Wood alerts us. We are prepared (I.13) for the further collapse of Macbeth's mind; we have not seen him since the first scene in Act Four.

Lady Macbeth. Here's the smell of the blood still: all the perfumes of Arabia will not sweeten this little hand. Oh! oh! oh!
Doctor. What a sigh is there! The heart is sorely charged.
Gentlewoman. I would not have such a heart in my bosom for the dignity of the whole body.
Doctor. Well, well, well.
Gentlewoman. Pray God it be, sir.
Doctor. This disease is beyond my practice: yet I have known those which have walked in their sleep who have died holily in their beds.
Lady Macbeth. Wash your hands, put on your night-gown; look not so pale. I tell you yet again, Banquo's buried; he cannot come out on 's grave.   67
Doctor. Even so?   68
Lady Macbeth. To bed, to bed: there's knocking at the gate. Come, come, come, come, give me your hand. What's done cannot be undone. To bed, to bed, to bed.
                              [*Exit.*

Doctor. Will she go now to bed?
Gentlewoman. Directly.
Doctor. Foul whisperings are abroad. Unnatural deeds
Do breed unnatural troubles; infected minds
To their deaf pillows will discharge their secrets;
More needs she the divine than the physician.
God, God forgive us all! Look after her;
Remove from her the means of all annoyance,   79
And still keep eyes upon her. So, good-night:
My mind she has mated, and amaz'd sight.   81
I think, but dare not speak.
Gentlewoman.   Good-night, good doctor. [*Exeunt.*

Scene two.

(THE COUNTRY NEAR DUNSINANE)

Enter, with drum and colours, MENTEITH, CAITHNESS, ANGUS, LENNOX, *and* Soldiers.
Menteith. The English power is near, led on by Malcolm,
His uncle Siward, and the good Macduff.   2
Revenges burn in them; for their dear causes   3
Would to the bleeding and the grim alarm   4
Excite the mortified man.
Angus.   Near Birnam wood
Shall we well meet them; that way are they coming.
Caithness. Who knows if Donalbain be with his brother?
Lennox. For certain, sir, he is not: I have a file
Of all the gentry: there is Siward's son,
And many unrough youths that even now
Protest their first of manhood.   11
Menteith.   What does the tyrant?
Caithness. Great Dunsinane he strongly fortifies.
Some say he's mad; others that lesser hate him
Do call it valiant fury; but, for certain,

67. "on's": of his.

68. "Even so?": The doctor has heard what amounts to a confession.

79. "means of all annoyance"; anything she might injure herself with.

81. "mated": baffled overcome (cf. checkmated, in chess).

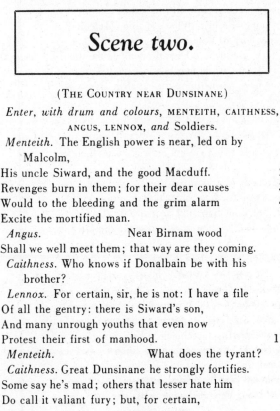

2. "uncle": Malcolm's mother was Siward's sister.

3. "dear": intense and personal.

4. "the bleeding . . . alarm": war.

4-5. "Would . . . man": would stir up even a man who had given up worldly action.

11. "Protest . . . manhood": for the first time show their manhood.

57

MACBETH

ACT V SCENE II

And the health/sickness symbolism (see above) is emphasized. The interesting thing is the degree of sympathy for Macbeth shown by these, his enemies, in lines 16-25.

The symbolism of the robe again sends our memories back to "borrowed robes," "strange garments," "Golden opinions worn," "old robes [that] sit easier than new" (I,iii,109-10, I,iii,145-6, I,vii,33-4, II,iv,38). Thus does verbal form come to the aid of the dramatic.

ACT V SCENE III

Macbeth's attendance by the doctor suggests his ill mind. In this and Scene Five he alternates wildly between furious ranting and quiet, weary melancholy. His soldierly common sense bids him fear, in the midst of which he clings to the false security of the prophecies.

In his quiet moods he is ripe for tragic self-awareness; his noisy moods, while expressing madness and the final outbursts of a destructive rage almost burnt out, at the same time are informed with a kind of valor. Lines like nine and ten ring with enough of the old warrior's courage to excite some admiration. His premature call for his armor shows both his desire for decisive action, and his longing for self-respect which he has known chiefly as a soldier in battle.

Tragic bitterness shows chiefly in ll.22-8, ll. 40-5, and ll.50-4, which passages reflect respectively his awareness of loneliness and enmity, remorse and self-disgust, his disastrous rule.

He cannot buckle his distemper'd cause 15
Within the belt of rule.
 Angus.   Now does he feel
His secret murders sticking on his hands; 17
Now minutely revolts upbraid his faith-breach; 18
Those he commands move only in command,
Nothing in love; now does he feel his title
Hang loose about him, like a giant's robe
Upon a dwarfish thief.
 Menteith.   Who then shall blame
His pester'd senses to recoil and start,
When all that is within him does condemn
Itself for being there?
 Caithness.   Well, march we on,
To give obedience where 'tis truly ow'd;
Meet we the medicine of the sickly weal,
And with him pour we in our country's purge
Each drop of us.
 Lennox. Or so much as it needs
To dew the sovereign flower and drown the weeds.
Make we our march towards Birnam.
       [*Exeunt, marching.*

Scene three.

(DUNSINANE. A ROOM IN THE CASTLE)

Enter MACBETH, Doctor, *and* Attendants.

Macbeth. Bring me no more reports; let them fly 1
 all:
Till Birnam wood remove to Dunsinane
I cannot taint with fear. What's the boy Malcolm?
Was he not born of woman? The spirits that know
All mortal consequences have pronounc'd me thus: 5
'Fear not, Macbeth; no man that's born of woman
Shall e'er have power upon thee.' Then fly, false
 thanes,
And mingle with the English epicures: 8
The mind I sway by and the heart I bear 9
Shall never sag with doubt nor shake with fear.

Enter a Servant.

The devil damn thee black, thou cream-fac'd loon! 11
Where gott'st thou that goose look?
Servant. There is ten thousand—
Macbeth.   Geese, villain?
Servant.   Soldiers, sir.
Macbeth. Go, prick thy face, and over-red thy fear,
Thou lily-liver'd boy. What soldiers, patch? 15
Death of thy soul! those linen cheeks of thine
Are counsellors to fear. What soldiers, whey-face? 17
Servant. The English force, so please you.
Macbeth. Take thy face hence. [*Exit Servant.*]
  Seyton!—I am sick at heart 19
When I behold—Seyton, I say!—This push 20
Will cheer me ever or disseat me now.
I have liv'd long enough: my way of life

15-6: "buckle . . . rule": bring order into his deranged affairs.

17. "sticking on his hands": i.e., as blood might.

18. "minutely": by the minute, every moment.

1. "them": the thanes.

5. "mortal consequences": the course of human events.

8. "epicures": luxury lovers, hence soft; from Epicurus, a Greek philosopher who believed that happiness was the goal of life. The English court was more civilized, cosmopolitan, and luxurious than the Scottish; therefore the English could be regarded contemptuously as playboys.

9. "sway": control the state, ironical in this context.

11. "loon" (or lown): a base and silly person.

15. "patch": fool.

17. "Are counsellors to fear": excite fear.
"whey": the watery part of milk.

19. "Seyton": This family were traditional armor-bearers to the Scottish kings.

"I am sick at heart" etc.: It seems most dramatic that these saner, and lower-keyed remarks should be addressed to the doctor.

MACBETH

ACT V SCENE III

Is fall'n into the sear, the yellow leaf; 23
And that which should accompany old age,
As honour, love, obedience, troops of friends, 25
I must not look to have; but, in their stead,
Curses, not loud but deep, mouth-honour, breath,
Which the poor heart would fain deny, and dare not. 28
Seyton!

Enter SEYTON.

Seyton. What is your gracious pleasure?
Macbeth.   What news more?
Seyton. All is confirm'd, my lord, which was
    reported.
Macbeth. I'll fight till from my bones my flesh be
    hack'd.
Give me my armour.
Seyton.   'Tis not needed yet.
Macbeth. I'll put it on.
Send out more horses, skirr the country round; 35
Hang those that talk of fear. Give me mine armour.
How does your patient, doctor?
Doctor.   Not so sick, my lord, 37
As she is troubled with thick-coming fancies, 38
That keep her from her rest.
Macbeth.   Cure her of that: 39
Canst thou not minister to a mind diseas'd,
Pluck from the memory a rooted sorrow,
Raze out the written troubles of the brain, 42
And with some sweet oblivious antidote 43
Cleanse the stuff'd bosom of that perilous stuff 44
Which weighs upon the heart?
Doctor.   Therein the patient
Must minister to himself.
Macbeth. Throw physic to the dogs; I'll none of it. 47
Come, put mine armour on; give me my staff. 48
Seyton, send out.—Doctor, the thanes fly from me.—
Come, sir, dispatch.—If thou could'st, doctor, cast 50
The water of my land, find her disease,
And purge it to a sound and pristine health, 52
I would applaud thee to the very echo,
That should applaud again.—Pull 't off, I say.— 54
What rhubarb, senna, or what purgative drug
Would scour these English hence? Hear'st thou of 56
    them?
Doctor. Ay, my good lord; your royal preparation
Makes us hear something.
Macbeth.   Bring it after me. 58
I will not be afraid of death and bane 59
Till Birnam forest come to Dunsinane.
Doctor. [*Aside.*] Were I from Dunsinane away and
    clear,
Profit again should hardly draw me here. [*Exeunt.*

23. "sear": dry, withered.

25. "As": such as.

28. "fain": like to.

35. "skirr": scour, ride rapidly.

37. "Not so sick": not so much afflicted with any bodily ailment.

38. "thick-coming fancies": many hallucinations.

39. "Cure . . . that": That is the very thing of which I wish you to cure her.

42. "Raze": take out, erase.

"written . . . brain": troubles written on the brain, remembered.

43. "oblivious": causing utter forgetfulness.

44. "the stuff'd bosom": The breathless, asthmatic quality of this line is most effective.

47. "I'll none of it": I'll have nothing to do with it.

48. "staff": baton (suggesting rank).

50. "dispatch": make haste.

50-1. "cast . . . water": diagnose; a medical figure from urine analysis.

52. "pristine": such as was enjoyed in former times.

54. "Pull't . . . say": some part of his armor.

56. "scour": clear away.

58. "Bring it after me": the piece of armor.

59. "bane": destruction, ruin.

59-62. The two rhyme tags are significant of the action. Each marks an exit: the first, Macbeth; the second, the Doctor.

MACBETH

ACT V SCENE IV

The scene is functional and spectacular, rather than intense or poetic. It shows us the meeting of Malcolm's supporters, the impatience of the old soldier, Siward, and the revenger, Macduff, and their plans to advance the war, and the means whereby the prophecy comes true. This incident of the hewing the boughs is taken from Holinshed. On stage it would be colorful and even festive with bright armor, banners, robes, and the green branches.

It is Shakespeare's usual technique, when leading up to a battle, to give a series of scenes alternately depicting the preparations of one side, then the other. By shortening them as the battle draws nearer, he builds up excitement and speed of movement towards the noisy climax. For the same method in use today, see the movies, where accelerated cutting from place to place fulfills the same function.

ACT V SCENE V

Herein Macbeth's gathering awareness almost completes itself, and the wish for death reaches its culmination. (For the death-wish, see III,ii and commentary, and comment to IV,iii,176-80.)

The soldiers are being mobilized to action stations on the walls, whence they would beat back attackers attempting to scale or pierce them.

His first realization here (ll. 9-15) is of his callous inhumanity, supped full with horrors" (cf. III, iv,142).

Scene four.

(COUNTRY NEAR BIRNAM WOOD)

Enter, with drum and colours, MALCOLM, *Old* SIWARD *and his* Son, MACDUFF, MENTEITH, CAITHNESS, ANGUS, LENNOX, ROSS, *and Soldiers marching.*

Malcolm. Cousins, I hope the days are near at hand
That chambers will be safe.
Menteith.   We doubt it nothing.   2
Siward. What wood is this before us?
Menteith. The wood of Birnam.
Malcolm.   Let every soldier hew him down a bough   5
And bear 't before him: thereby shall we shadow
The numbers of our host, and make discovery   7
Err in report of us.
Soldiers.   It shall be done.
Siward. We learn no other but the confident tyrant   9
Keeps still in Dunsinane, and will endure   10
Our setting down before 't.   11
Malcolm.   'Tis his main hope;
For where there is advantage to be given,   12
Both more and less have given him the revolt,   13
And none serve with him but constrained things   14
Whose hearts are absent too.
Macduff.   Let our just censures   15
Attend the true event, and put we on   16
Industrious soldiership.
Siward.   The time approaches
That will with due decision make us know
What we shall say we have and what we owe.
Thoughts speculative, their unsure hopes relate,   20
But certain issue strokes must arbitrate,   21
Towards which advance the war.   22
                 [*Exeunt, marching.*

Scene five.

(DUNSINANE. WITHIN THE CASTLE)

Enter, with a drum and colours, MACBETH, SEYTON, *and* Soldiers.

Macbeth. Hang out our banners on the
    outward walls;   1
The cry is still, 'They come;' our castle's strength   2
Will laugh a siege to scorn; here let them lie   3
Till famine and the ague eat them up;   4
Were they not forc'd with those that should be ours,   5
We might have met them dareful, beard to beard,   6
And beat them backward home.
            [*A cry of women within.*
            What is that noise?

The Scottish nobles have now joined forces with Malcolm at Birnam Wood.

2. "That chambers will be safe": meaning safe from murderers, etc.

     "nothing": not at all.

5. "Let every" etc.: This stratagem is a very old piece of popular fiction, widespread in folktales, and appears in Holinshed's account of the battle.

7. "discovery": Macbeth's scouts.

9. "no other": nothing else.

11. "setting down": encampment for siege.

12. where there is an opportunity for deserting.

13. "more and less": high and low, great and small.

14. "constrained things": those who are forced to.

15-7. "Let our . . . soldiership": Save our talk till after the battle; in the meantime fight like good soldiers.

15. "just censures": good judgments.

16. "Attend": wait for.

     "the true event": what really happens.

20-1. Calculations state our reasonable but unsure hopes; only battle will produce results (echoing McDuff's impatience, ll. 15-7).

22. "Towards which": towards the result of the battle.

1. "outward walls": The castle had various walls and fortifications which had to be taken one after the other.

2. "still": always.

3. "lie": lie encamped.

4. "ague": fever.

5. "forc'd": strengthened, reinforced.

6. "met them": in the field.
     "dareful": boldly.

MACBETH

ACT V SCENE V

Lady Macbeth's death is pathetic but not heroic (see V,vii,98-100). It prompts his famous denunciation of life, a realization of the vanity of human ambition in sharpest contrast with the sentiment of "We'd jump the life to come" (I,vii,6-7). The reflection whets his appetite for death in order to be rid of his bitter time ("Out, out, brief candle" [l. 23] and cf. "life's fitful fever" [III,ii, 23]).

Then, immediately, the news of Birnam Wood, brings him partial realization of the way the apparitions have duped and mocked him. His reaction is twofold, a melancholy call upon death and chaos, then a burst of valiant fury leading towards the solace of violent action.

Seyton. It is the cry of women, my good lord. [*Exit.* 8
Macbeth. I have almost forgot the taste of fears. 9
The time has been my senses would have cool'd 10
To hear a night-shriek, and my fell of hair 11
Would at a dismal treatise rouse and stir 12
As life were in 't. I have supp'd full with horrors;
Direness, familiar to my slaughterous thoughts, 14
Cannot once start me.

Re-enter SEYTON.

　　　　Wherefore was that cry?
Seyton. The queen, my lord, is dead.
Macbeth. She should have died hereafter; 17
There would have been a time for such a word. 18
To-morrow, and to-morrow, and to-morrow,
Creeps in this petty pace from day to day,
To the last syllable of recorded time; 21
And all our yesterdays have lighted fools
The way to dusty death. Out, out, brief candle! 23
Life's but a walking shadow, a poor player
That struts and frets his hour upon the stage, 25
And then is heard no more; it is a tale
Told by an idiot, full of sound and fury,
Signifying nothing. 28

Enter a Messenger.

Thou com'st to use thy tongue; thy story quickly.
Messenger. Gracious my lord, 30
I should report that which I say I saw,
But know not how to do it.
Macbeth. 　　　　Well, say, sir.
Messenger. As I did stand my watch upon the hill, 33
I look'd towards Birnam, and anon, methought,
The wood began to move.
Macbeth. 　　　　Liar and slave!
Messenger. Let me endure your wrath if 't be
　　not so;
Within this three mile you may see it coming; 37
I say, a moving grove.
Macbeth. 　　　　If thou speak'st false, 38
Upon the next tree shalt thou hang alive,
Till famine cling thee; if thy speech be sooth, 40
I care not if thou dost for me as much.
I pull in resolution and begin 42
To doubt the equivocation of the fiend 43
That lies like truth; 'Fear not, till Birnam wood
Do come to Dunsinane;' and now a wood
Comes toward Dunsinane. Arm, arm, and out!
If this which he avouches does appear, 47
There is nor flying hence, nor tarrying here.
I 'gin to be aweary of the sun, 49
And wish the estate o' the world were now undone. 50
Ring the alarum-bell! Blow, wind! come, wrack! 51
At least we'll die with harness on our back. 52
　　　　　　　　　　[*Exeunt.*

8. "It . . . women": Seyton hurries out to learn the reason for the women's shrieks.

9. "forgot the taste of fears": forgotten what dreadful things are like.

10. "cool'd": felt the chill of terror.

11. "fell": scalp, skin.

12. "treatise": story.

14. "Direness": horror.

17. "should": means (as very often) inevitably or certainly would.

18. "such a word": meaning "death."

21. "recorded time": time as measured in human history.

23. "brief candle": life is compared to a candle flame.

25. "struts and frets": Macbeth's contempt for human life.

28. "Signifying nothing": lacking sense or meaning.

30. "Gracious my lord": my gracious lord.

33. "As I did stand my watch": while being on duty.

37. "mile": an old form of the plural.

38. "I say": The messenger is courageous: he repeats the terrible message to his face.

40. "Till famine cling thee": till you waste away and your skin sticks to your bones.
"sooth": truth.

42. "pull in": restrain.

43. "To . . . fiend": to suspect Satan of ambiguous prophecies.

47. "avouches": vouches for, says is true.

"appear": i.e., to our sight.

49. "gin": begin.

50. "estate": settled order.

"undone": returned to chaos.

51. "wrack": destruction, wreck, ruin.

52. "harness": armor.

MACBETH

ACT V SCENE VI

Attention should be paid to the spectacle that fills this little scene out: the flags, the martial business, the motion as the green boughs go down, the braying of trumpets.

ACT V SCENE VII

Haggard Macbeth has still to have his last delusion (of charmed life) stripped from him; until then he fights with a courage that is partly the remains of his rage, partly desperation, partly posturing in the likeness of "Bellona's bridegroom" (I,ii,55).

Bear-baiting was a popular spectacle in Elizabethan times. A bear-baiting arena was almost next door to the Globe theater, and the outside of the buildings was so alike, that in several old maps and views their names were erroneously switched. In this sport, a bear, tied to a stake in the center of the arena, was exposed to the attacks of a pack of dogs until either it or they were killed.

Scene six.

(THE SAME. A PLAIN BEFORE THE CASTLE)

Enter, with drum and colours, MALCOLM, *Old* SIWARD, MACDUFF, *&c., and their Army, with boughs.*

Malcolm. Now near enough; your leavy screens throw down,   1
And show like those you are. You, worthy uncle,   2
Shall, with my cousin, your right-noble son,
Lead our first battle; worthy Macduff and we   4
Shall take upon 's what else remains to do,   5
According to our order.   6
  Siward.   Fare you well.
Do we but find the tyrant's power to-night,   7
Let us be beaten, if we cannot fight.
  Macduff. Make all our trumpets speak; give them all breath,
Those clamorous harbingers of blood and death.   10
                           [Exeunt.

Scene seven.

(THE SAME. ANOTHER PART OF THE PLAIN)

Alarums. Enter MACBETH

Macbeth. They have tied me to a stake; I cannot fly,   1
But bear-like I must fight the course. What's he   2
That was not born of woman? Such a one
Am I to fear, or none.
        Enter Young SIWARD.
Young Siward. What is thy name?
  Macbeth.   Thou'lt be afraid to hear it.   5
Young Siward. No; though thou call'st thyself a hotter name
Than any is in hell.
  Macbeth.   My name's Macbeth.
Young Siward. The devil himself could not pronounce a title
More hateful to mine ear.
  Macbeth.   No, nor more fearful.
Young Siward. Thou liest, abhorred tyrant; with my sword
I'll prove the lie thou speak'st.
      [They fight and Young SIWARD *is slain.*
  Macbeth.   Thou wast born of woman:
But swords I smile at, weapons laugh to scorn,
Brandish'd by man that's of a woman born.   *[Exit.*
      Alarums. Enter MACDUFF.
Macduff. That way the noise is. Tyrant, show thy face:
If thou be'st slain and with no stroke of mine,
My wife and children's ghosts will haunt me still.   16
I cannot strike at wretched kerns, whose arms   17
Are hir'd to bear their staves: either thou, Macbeth,   18
Or else my sword with an unbatter'd edge
I sheathe again undeeded. There thou should'st be;   20

1. "leavy": leafy.

2. "show": appear.
   "worthy": noble.

4. "battle": division.

   "we": Malcolm here assumes the royal plural for the first time.

5. "what": whatever.

6. "our order": the plans already made.

7. "Do we": if we do.
   "power": forces.

10. "harbingers": messengers.

1. "They . . . stake": a figure from bear-baiting. A bear was tied to a stake and attacked by dogs.

2. "course": one bout.

5. The encounter with young Siward adds suspense because it encourages Macbeth to trust "the fiend" still.

16. "still": ever, forever.

17. "kerns": light-armed soldiers.

18. "staves": spears, lances.

20. "undeeded": unused.
    "should'st be": ought to be, to judge by the din.

MACBETH

ACT V SCENE VII

ACT V SCENE VIII

Macbeth's rejection of suicide shows that the idea has crossed his mind before.

As the last prophecy collapses, Macbeth can recognize how completely he has been misled; he knows what we know. Thus stripped to the very bed-rock of existence, his will comes to a dead stop ("I'll not fight with thee"). There is no desire now, only bitterness. It requires Macduff's taunt to arouse the last of his warlike pride before he will "fight the course" and "die with harness on his back."

By this great clatter, one of greatest note 21
Seems bruited. Let me find him, fortune! 22
And more I beg not. [*Exit. Alarums.*

Enter MALCOLM *and Old* SIWARD.

Siward. This way, my lord; the castle's
gently render'd: 24
The tyrant's people on both sides do fight;
The noble thanes do bravely in the war; 26
The day almost itself professes yours, 27
And little is to do.
Malcolm. We have met with foes
That strike beside us.
Siward. Enter, sir, the castle. [*Exeunt. Alarums.* 29

Scene eight.

(THE SAME. ANOTHER PART OF THE PLAIN)

Re-enter MACBETH.

Macbeth. Why should I play the Roman fool, and
die 1
On mine own sword? whiles I see lives, the gashes 2
Do better upon them.

Re-enter MACDUFF.

Macduff. Turn, hell-hound, turn!
Macbeth. Of all men else I have avoided thee: 4
But get thee back, my soul is too much charg'd
With blood of thine already.
Macduff. I have no words;
My voice is in my sword, thou bloodier villain
Than terms can give thee out! [*They fight*
Macbeth. Thou losest labour: 8
As easy mayst thou the intrenchant air 9
With thy keen sword impress as make me bleed: 10
Let fall thy blade on vulnerable crests;
I bear a charmed life, which must not yield 12
To one of woman born.
Macduff. Despair thy charm;
And let the angel whom thou still hast serv'd 14
Tell thee, Macduff was from his mother's womb
Untimely ripp'd.
Macbeth. Accursed be that tongue that tells me so,
For it hath cow'd my better part of man: 18
And be these juggling fiends no more believ'd,
That palter with us in a double sense; 20
That keep the word of promise to our ear,
And break it to our hope. I'll not fight with thee. 22
Macduff. Then yield thee, coward,
And live to be the show and gaze o' the time: 24
We'll have thee, as our rarer monsters are,
Painted upon a pole, and underwrit, 26
'Here may you see the tyrant.'
Macbeth. I will not yield,
To kiss the ground before young Malcolm's feet,
And to be baited with the rabble's curse. 29
Though Birnam wood be come to Dunsinane,
And thou oppos'd, being of no woman born,
Yet I will try the last: before my body 32

21. "one": someone.
    "note": rank.

22. "bruited": reported, proclaimed.

24. "gently render'd": surrendered without resistance.

26. "bravely": finely, splendidly.

27. "itself professes yours": calls itself yours.

29. "beside us": so as to miss us.

---

1. It was proper for Roman officers to commit suicide rather than surrender.

2. "lives": those who are living.

4. "avoided thee": Macbeth is avoiding Macduff not only because of the Beware Macduff prophecy but because he feels sure that Macduff will fall if they fight, and he has still a drop of the "milk of human kindness" left.

8. "Than . . . out": than words can describe thee.

9. "intrenchant": that cannot be cut or gashed.

10. "impress": make an impression on.

12-13. "bear . . . born": He wants Macduff to yield; he doesn't wish to kill him.

14. "angel": demon, guarding spirit.

18. "my better . . . man": my courage.

20. "palter": deal deceitfully, equivocate.

22. "I'll . . . thee": Macbeth feels helplessly abandoned by the Fates.

24. "gaze'" spectacle.
    "time": age.

26. "Painted upon a pole": painted on canvas and fastened to a pole (as at a circus).

29. "baited": assailed, tormented.

32. "the last": i.e., strength and valor, which may yet prove stronger than fate.

63

MACBETH

ACT V SCENE VIII

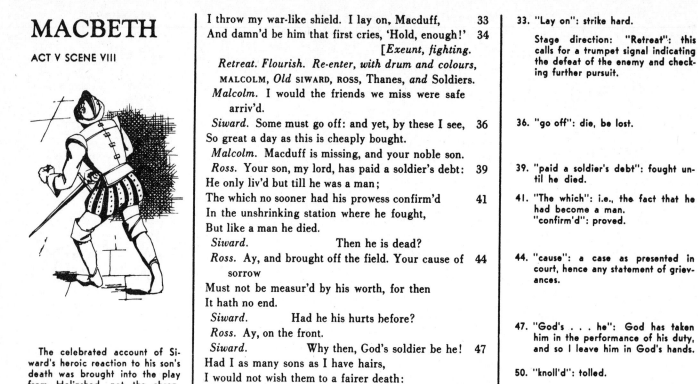

The celebrated account of Siward's heroic reaction to his son's death was brought into the play from Holinshed, not the chronicle of Macbeth, but that of Edward the Confessor in the volumes devoted to English history. It will be recalled that Siward, too, was King James's ancestor.

The play ends in a sense of blessed release from tyranny, and the promise of health and order restored by the rightful king, who in assuming his task calls upon the grace of God.

I throw my war-like shield. I lay on, Macduff, 33
And damn'd be him that first cries, 'Hold, enough!' 34
         [Exeunt, fighting.
Retreat. Flourish. Re-enter, with drum and colours,
MALCOLM, *Old* SIWARD, ROSS, Thanes, *and* Soldiers.
Malcolm. I would the friends we miss were safe
 arriv'd.
Siward. Some must go off: and yet, by these I see, 36
So great a day as this is cheaply bought.
Malcolm. Macduff is missing, and your noble son.
Ross. Your son, my lord, has paid a soldier's debt: 39
He only liv'd but till he was a man;
The which no sooner had his prowess confirm'd 41
In the unshrinking station where he fought,
But like a man he died.
Siward.   Then he is dead?
Ross. Ay, and brought off the field. Your cause of 44
 sorrow
Must not be measur'd by his worth, for then
It hath no end.
Siward.   Had he his hurts before?
Ross. Ay, on the front.
Siward.   Why then, God's soldier be he! 47
Had I as many sons as I have hairs,
I would not wish them to a fairer death:
And so, his knell is knoll'd. 50
Malcolm.   He's worth more sorrow,
And that I'll spend for him.
Siward.   He's worth no more;
They say he parted well, and paid his score: 52
And so, God be with him! Here comes newer
 comfort.
    Re-enter MACDUFF, *with* MACBETH's *head.*
Macduff. Hail, king! for so thou art. Behold,
 where stands
The usurper's cursed head: the time is free: 55
I see thee compass'd with thy kingdom's pearl, 56
That speak my salutation in their minds;
Whose voices I desire aloud with mine;
Hail, King of Scotland!
All.   Hail, King of Scotland!
             [Flourish.
Malcolm. We shall not spend a large expense of
 time
Before we reckon with your several loves, 61
And make us even with you. My thanes and
 kinsmen,
Henceforth be earls, the first that ever Scotland
In such an honour nam'd. What's more to do, 64
Which would be planted newly with the time, 65
As calling home our exil'd friends abroad
That fled the snares of watchful tyranny;
Producing forth the cruel ministers 68
Of this dead butcher and his fiend-like queen,
Who, as 'tis thought, by self and violent hands
Took off her life; this, and what needful else 71
That calls upon us, by the grace of Grace 72
We will perform in measure, time, and place: 73
So, thanks to all at once and to each one, 74
Whom we invite to see us crown'd at Scone.
         [Flourish. Exeunt.

33. "Lay on": strike hard.

 Stage direction: "Retreat": this calls for a trumpet signal indicating the defeat of the enemy and checking further pursuit.

36. "go off": die, be lost.

39. "paid a soldier's debt": fought until he died.

41. "The which": i.e., the fact that he had become a man.
"confirm'd": proved.

44. "cause": a case as presented in court, hence any statement of grievances.

47. "God's . . . he": God has taken him in the performance of his duty, and so I leave him in God's hands.

50. "knoll'd": tolled.

52. "parted well": made a good end, owed nothing.

55. "the time is free": Now we are free (from tyranny).

56. "compass'd": surrounded.
"pearl": all that's good in the kingdom.

61. "reckon with": repay.

64. "What's more to do": whatever else must be done.

65. "Which . . . time": that the new order of things requires.

68. "Producing forth": bringing to light or justice.

71. "what needful else": whatever else is necessary.

72. "calls upon us": demands my attention.

73. "in measure": with propriety and decorum as opposed to the crude rule of Macbeth.

74-5. "one . . . Scone": They make a very good rhyme in the English of Shakespeare's time.

NOTES

NOTES

NOTES

NOTES

NOTES